TEST
DECADE
1972/1982

TEST DECADE
1972/1982

Photographs and captions by
Patrick Eagar

Text by Graeme Wright

WORLD'S WORK LTD

Design by Victor Shreeve

Photographs copyright © 1982 by Patrick Eagar

Text copyright © 1982 by Graeme Wright

Published by World's Work Ltd.,
The Windmill Press, Kingswood, Tadworth, Surrey

Printed in Great Britain by
Hazell, Watson & Viney Ltd., Aylesbury, Bucks.

SBN 437 04050 X

To my mother

CONTENTS

8 — 11	INTRODUCTION
1972/73	*1st Test* **England v. Australia** *Old Trafford* *2nd Test* **England v. Australia** *Lord's* *3rd Test* **England v. Australia** *Trent Bridge* *4th Test* **England v. Australia** *Headingley* *5th Test* **England v. Australia** *The Oval*
12 — 29	*2nd Test* **West Indies v. Australia** *Bridgetown* *3rd Test* **West Indies v. Australia** *Port of Spain*
1973/74	*1st Test* **England v. New Zealand** *Trent Bridge* *2nd Test* **England v. New Zealand** *Lord's* *3rd Test* **England v. New Zealand** *Headingley*
30 — 43	*1st Test* **England v. West Indies** *The Oval* *2nd Test* **England v. West Indies** *Edgbaston* *3rd Test* **England v. West Indies** *Lord's*
1974/75	*1st Test* **England v. India** *Old Trafford* *2nd Test* **England v. India** *Lord's* *3rd Test* **England v. India** *Edgbaston*
	1st Test **England v. Pakistan** *Headingley* *2nd Test* **England v. Pakistan** *Lord's* *3rd Test* **England v. Pakistan** *The Oval*
44 — 63	*2nd Test* **Australia v. England** *Perth* *3rd Test* **Australia v. England** *Melbourne* *4th Test* **Australia v. England** *Sydney*
1975/76	*1st Test* **England v. Australia** *Edgbaston* *2nd Test* **England v. Australia** *Lord's* *3rd Test* **England v. Australia** *Headingley* *4th Test* **England v. Australia** *The Oval*
64 — 83	*1st Test* **Australia v. West Indies** *Brisbane* *2nd Test* **Australia v. West Indies** *Perth* *3rd Test* **Australia v. West Indies** *Melbourne* *4th Test* **Australia v. West Indies** *Sydney*
1976/77	*1st Test* **England v. West Indies** *Trent Bridge* *2nd Test* **England v. West Indies** *Lord's* *3rd Test* **England v. West Indies** *Old Trafford* *4th Test* **England v. West Indies** *Headingley* *5th Test* **England v. West Indies** *The Oval*
	2nd Test **India v. England** *Calcutta* *3rd Test* **India v. England** *Madras*
84 — 109	*Centenary Test* **Australia v. England** *Melbourne*

1977/78

1st Test England v. Australia *Lord's*
2nd Test England v. Australia *Old Trafford*
3rd Test England v. Australia *Trent Bridge*
4th Test England v. Australia *Headingley*
5th Test England v. Australia *The Oval*

3rd Test Pakistan v. England *Karachi*

1st Test West Indies v. Australia *Port of Spain*
2nd Test West Indies v. Australia *Bridgetown*

110 — 129

1978/79

1st Test England v. Pakistan *Edgbaston*
2nd Test England v. Pakistan *Lord's*
3rd Test England v. Pakistan *Headingley*

1st Test England v. New Zealand *The Oval*
2nd Test England v. New Zealand *Trent Bridge*
3rd Test England v. New Zealand *Lord's*

2nd Test Pakistan v. India *Lahore*

2nd Test Australia v. England *Perth*
3rd Test Australia v. England *Melbourne*
4th Test Australia v. England *Sydney*

130 — 153

1979/80

1st Test England v. India *Edgbaston*
2nd Test England v. India *Lord's*
3rd Test England v. India *Headingley*
4th Test England v. India *The Oval*

2nd Test Australia v. England *Sydney*
3rd Test Australia v. West Indies *Adelaide*
3rd Test Australia v. England *Melbourne*

Jubilee Test India v. England *Bombay*

154 — 171

1980/81

1st Test England v. West Indies *Trent Bridge*
2nd Test England v. West Indies *Lord's*
3rd Test England v. West Indies *Old Trafford*
4th Test England v. West Indies *The Oval*
5th Test England v. West Indies *Headingley*

Centenary Test England v. Australia *Lord's*

1st Test West Indies v. England *Port of Spain*
2nd Test West Indies v. England *Georgetown*
3rd Test West Indies v. England *Bridgetown*

172 — 195

1981/82

1st Test England v. Australia *Trent Bridge*
2nd Test England v. Australia *Lord's*
3rd Test England v. Australia *Headingley*
4th Test England v. Australia *Edgbaston*
5th Test England v. Australia *Old Trafford*
6th Test England v. Australia *The Oval*

1st Test India v. England *Bombay*

3rd Test Australia v. Pakistan *Melbourne*

196 — 219

222   INDEX

INTRODUCTION

"Hey, guv – d'yer photograph every ball?" asked the small Essex lad, as he poked his face into the far end of my lens just at the moment John Lever bowled. It is a question asked many times a day during the cricket season, though it is not always asked in quite such a direct manner.

The answer, had I been more polite, would have been that, though I watch and concentrate all the time, to photograph every ball, in hope, would be wasteful in the extreme. Very fast reactions are less important than a good sense of timing. After all, a batsman facing Michael Holding has far less time to defend his body or his wicket than the photographer, who has only to record the effect of the batsman's mistakes. A stump, cart-wheeling 18 yards, may be airborne for a few seconds, while the 90 m.p.h. cricket ball travels the length of the pitch in under half a second. Photographing a flying stump is comparatively simple.

It is a waiting game, and it can be very frustrating if nothing much is happening. *The Sunday Times* picture desk often wonder what I have been up to all morning, when only a few pictures have been taken by lunchtime. On the other hand, a particularly hectic over, one when a wicket or two falls, could result in a roll or more of film being exposed in a few minutes. Modern cameras can take up to six photographs every second (until the film runs out), and if two or more cameras are linked together film can be consumed at an alarming rate.

These very high speeds are just one of many technical developments of the last 10 years. At the other extreme it is only in the last couple of seasons that the last two 'long tom' cameras in regular use have been retired. In use since the end of the First World War, these cameras used lenses originally designed for photo-reconnaissance from airships, and often salvaged from those that had been shot down. Herbert Fishwick, the Australian photographer, imported one specially from England and used it for many years. It was with this type of camera that he took the famous photograph of Hammond's cover drive at Sydney in 1928. Other notable images made with the 'long tom' include Ron Lovitt's of the tied Test at Brisbane. However beautiful their results, they were exceedingly bulky cameras, slow to use and awkward to carry around.

Some considerable relief greeted Dennis Oulds' decision to stop using his in 1980. After a personal career in cricket photography going back to Trent Bridge in 1934, he declared his camera beyond reasonable repair and settled for something smaller. The knack had been never to arrive at a cricket ground at the same time as Dennis, or you might be persuaded into helping him hump the overweight, coffin-like contraption to what was usually the highest point on the ground. Once installed, each plate had to be loaded into the camera by hand, a time-consuming operation which ensured that no more than three photographs an over were possible, except of course for those bowled at the currently accepted rate by the fastest bowlers playing today.

The last 10 years have seen some remarkable changes in the design of cameras and lenses. Accelerated by the US space and defence programme, the development of the microchip has given us cameras that are controlled by microprocessors, shutters that are timed to quartz-clock accuracy and the whole run on batteries as small as buttons which have the unfortunate tendency to run out at inconvenient moments. Ever since computers were used to design lenses the quality has continued to improve dramatically; new types of glass have been dreamt up; and in terms of quality and convenience, cricket photographers have never had it so good.

The film manufacturers have played their part too. The range and quality of the materials available have made the production of good quality photographs (especially colour) easier than ever before. I remember that in 1972, provided the conditions were favourable, it was possible to take good close up action colour photographs. This usually depended on brilliant sunshine – not always the best light for the most flattering photographs; otherwise it was a question of using the fastest films available and suffering a somewhat second-rate result.

One piece of equipment that I have found especially useful is a gadget for taking photographs by remote control, over distances of up to half a mile away. Certainly the far side of any cricket ground is well within range. Using one or more of these units, it is possible to photograph the same moment from two or more different angles – and one is always better than the others. This then gives the photographer some of the choice available to the TV producer who, currently in Australia, can select from the images of up to a dozen instant replay electronic eyes. Many of the photographs in this book were taken in this way. A major problem can be the decision, in a split second, of which of the many buttons available to press – I have missed some important moments by hesitating just too long.

Ten years ago, while in an early experimental stage, I tried to do something similar – but using five hundred feet of electric cable. It took most of the morning to set it up, trailing the wire from the midwicket area, around the boundary and up a BBC television tower to the top, where it was attached to one of my cameras. It was not a success. I think nearly half the spectators in Maidstone that day must have tripped over the wire – happily no twisted ankles were reported. I had trouble in persuading the television cameramen and technicians that although the camera was unattended it was actually working. I took a number of photographs of the back of their heads when they had moved in front of it, and then, when one of them helpfully moved it to a safer place, I spent the remainder of the afternoon recording some excellent cloud studies.

Since then I have had a happy relationship with the BBC and they have been frequent custodians of my remote control cameras.

Before 1972 Test matches were photographed exclusively by one of two agencies who distributed their photographs to all who might want them. However it did mean that everyone received the same photographs and, in Fleet Street, where the word exclusive is all important, picture editors found little encouragement to publish photographs of Test cricket knowing that the same photograph was likely to be used by their rivals. I had already been photographing county cricket for a number of years, but had not, until that time, been officially allowed to take a single photograph of a Test match. In fact I had begun to despair that my only hope would be to work overseas.

The 1972 Ashes series in England was my first, and it was as a result of an experiment by the Test and County Cricket Board that allowed a limited number of photographers in to cover Test matches. That is where this book starts. It was Dennis Lillee's summer and the re-emergence of cricket as a spectator sport in England. For some years interest, and crowds, had been declining. While photographers could not claim all the credit, one cannot help feeling that the extensive picture coverage given to that series in Fleet Street and in the specialist cricket press must have contributed something. There were teething troubles – the passes issued to photographers at Trent Bridge were clearly endorsed 'Photography strictly forbidden'. Happily the experiment was

Michael Holding, who has been timed at over 90mph, uproots Underwood's leg stump. The photographer has a simpler job than the batsman in this sort of situation, but it requires a high degree of concentration and readiness to get it right.

adjudged a success, and we were allowed back to photograph the next year's series against New Zealand and the West Indies. Since then I have not missed a single Test match in England.

Along with matches from Australia, West Indies, India and Pakistan this book is my record of an eventful 10 years. Altogether there are 81 Test matches (not including the unhappy expedition to Guyana in 1981 – still known as the 2nd Test, but more likely to be remembered as The Jackman Affair).

Conditions for photographer and spectator, not to mention the player, vary enormously from country to country. It is hard to attempt any photography of the crowds in the West Indies without becoming involved in a profound and detailed discussion of the playing careers of all the England players, their recent successes and failures, their strengths and their weaknesses. It is also difficult to avoid the copious quantities of rum, generously offered and sparingly refused (at risk of giving offence). I once enjoyed the most soporific of afternoons at Port of Spain, having spent a couple of hours on what I had mistakenly assumed would be a few minutes' mission into one of the public stands in the heat of the midday sun. I had previously been

warned (in another territory of the Caribbean) that such an outing might not be wise, and that I would be safer if I stayed in the members' area.

By comparison, both India and Pakistan can be altogether more violent. No rum is allowed into the grounds here, but I was once hit hard by a well aimed apple in Calcutta while attempting to photograph the police removing two over-enthusiastic students from one of the stands. I was also, fortunately, missed by a bottle or two in Lahore while taking an ill advised walk round the boundary during a particularly dull session of play. The enthusiasm is so great that events can easily get out of hand – caution and moderation are essential.

A pommie photographer is fair game on the Hill at Sydney or in the far reaches of the 'outer' at Melbourne – excursions there are best carried out with discretion at all times and hardly at all after four o'clock in the afternoon.

The lighting too, can impose problems. In the West Indies and Australia the high overhead sun is often too harsh for the best results; and while the players may feel comfortable in their wide brimmed hats, they do nothing to help what little light can reach their faces. It can be a little softer on the Indian subcontinent where Test matches are played in the coolest part of the year, when the sun is at its lowest. The soft, diffused light, so often encountered during the English summer months

A sequence of Dennis Lillee in action taken in 1980. At the end of the ten year period he had taken 321 Test wickets – 12 more than Lance Gibbs.

is ideal for cricket photography, and I find that usually the best photographs are taken in England.

Photographers do not get a second chance. The good action photograph is the product of an instant; the instant missed is a photograph gone for ever. Our colleagues with the typewriters, do, on a moment to moment basis, get second chances. A powerful lobby group, some years ago they successfully applied for television sets in the press box. The television instant replay gives aid and comfort for those who have their heads down at the typewriter, or who are unfavourably positioned to see the nuances of a particular stroke or dismissal.

On the first day of the High Court hearing in the Packer case I decided to try to photograph Tony Greig and Kerry Packer together as they left the court. They had arrived separately and there was every chance that they would leave separately — even by different exits. I arrived well before the end of the first day's hearing and loitered around the main entrance in the way I imagined the court photographers did, my camera dangling from my neck. As the time approached for the adjournment of the day's proceedings, I was congratulating myself that if Greig and Packer emerged together, the scoop would be mine — there were no other photographers in sight. Imagine my delight when I saw that they were together, and were heading in my direction.

I had reckoned without the guile and experience of Fleet Street. Suddenly I was surrounded by half a dozen photographers, who had appeared as if from nowhere, small pocketable and expendable cameras at the ready. This group must have had me under amused surveillance for some time, and wondered what sort of twit was trying to do their job without the most elementary precautions — learnt from experience of reluctant divorcees and evasive criminals. As Greig and Packer drew nearer, they were now within lens range. Tony Greig then walked straight up to me and said, "Hello Patrick, have you met Kerry?" It's not easy to shake hands and take photographs simultaneously — I did my best; and at the same time spoilt half a dozen other photographers' shots.

Fortunately one doesn't have to be quite as close to the action as that all the time — and hopefully cricket will never again have to fight its battles in the High Court.

My thanks go to Graeme Wright, who in the sections that follow, has skilfully told the story of the decade — the events leading up to and following the 1977 watershed. My thanks, also, to Jan Traylen for making every print in the book — at times a trying experience, especially from the earlier negatives — and for his help over the years.

PE

1972/73

1st Test **England v. Australia** *Old Trafford*
2nd Test **England v. Australia** *Lord's*
3rd Test **England v. Australia** *Trent Bridge*
4th Test **England v. Australia** *Headingley*
5th Test **England v. Australia** *The Oval*

2nd Test **West Indies v. Australia** *Bridgetown*
3rd Test **West Indies v. Australia** *Port of Spain*

'When he bowled his first ball in front of a crowd that had not seen him bowl before, there was a corporate gasp which told more than many words.' So wrote John Arlott of Dennis Lillee following the 1972 series between England and Australia. The six-feet tall, broad-shouldered Australian fast bowler, whose ferocious approach to the wicket over a 44-pace run-in preceded a thunderbolt delivery, had undermined the confidence of every batsman who faced him in those Test matches, and his presence alone had attracted thousands anxious to witness the bowler who, without question, was the fastest in the world.

Great batsmen in full flow draw the breath from a crowd marvelling at their strokes, but little can compare with the hush that envelops a ground as the truly fast bowler turns at his mark and breaks into his run. No one, batsman or spectator, knows what plan is in his mind. It is a moment of suspense, a drama enacted six times in an over, and when the central character wears his dark hair long and his moustache falling around his lips like a Mexican revolutionary, that drama is heightened to the extent that he is more than an athlete. He is an actor in possession of a stage.

When he first arrived in England, it was that moustache which drew attention to Lillee, more than his prowess as a fast bowler. Facial plumage was the vanity of the footballer and the pop-star, not of a cricketer. Lillee had, it was remembered, taken five wickets in an innings on his Test début in January 1971 against England, but the fast bowling hero of that series was John Snow. Moody, hostile, Snow and opening batsman Geoffrey Boycott had played the leading roles as England regained the Ashes under Ray Illingworth. Since then, Lillee had proved susceptible to back injury, owing to his demanding delivery action, and in the cold, wet early English summer of 1972 there were real fears that this problem would end his career prematurely.

By June, however, Lillee was considered fit for the first Test at Old Trafford; Massie, his fellow Western Australian opening bowler, was not, leaving Australia without the man best suited to exploit the conditions. Yet England, after the first day, were just 147 for five – and the Australians had missed four catches and a run-out. Lillee was simply too fast for English batsmen grown accustomed to a diet of medium-pace seam-up, while Gleeson, with his unorthodox spin, was too complicated for them. Not even Boycott, England's master batsman, could cope, retiring hurt after being hit on the arm by Lillee. Only Edrich and Greig gave any semblance of tenure, and a total of 249 was more than England could have hoped for. But when Snow and Arnold cut a swathe through Australia's batting, England were a match-winning 107 ahead. Greig again top-scored in England's second innings, while Lillee's six for 66 confirmed his reputation. Left to score 342, Australia looked well beaten at 147 for eight, and only a lusty 91 from the left-handed wicket-keeper, Marsh, reduced the margin of defeat to 89 runs. Snow, with another four wickets, matched Lillee with eight wickets for the match.

Massie returned for the Lord's Test to share the new ball and found the heavy atmosphere swing bowlers dream of. In England's first innings he took eight for 84, in the second eight for 53. Lillee accounted for the other four batsmen and only Greig passed 50 for England – his third half-century of the series. Greg Chappell's elegant hundred, supported by fifties from his brother Ian, Australia's captain, and Marsh, saw Australia put on 308 in their first innings. In the second, the fast-scoring Stackpole hit 57 of the 81 Australia required for victory and the fight for the Ashes was wide open.

A near-perfect pitch at Trent Bridge allowed England's batsmen to secure a draw after Chappell had given them a target of 451 and his bowlers some 570 minutes to bowl them out. But it was an anything-but-perfect wicket at Headingley which made Underwood's medium-pace spin virtually unplayable and won England the fourth Test by nine wickets in three days. Only Stackpole, and to some degree Sheahan, overcame the conditions, whereas England's batsmen had less to fear from the slower turn of Mallett and Inverarity as they mustered 263. Australia could manage only 146 and 136 as Underwood celebrated his Test recall with match figures of 10 for 82.

An official report on the pitch laid the blame on a disease called 'fusarium' that killed most of the grass while the pitch was covered during the heavy storms prior to the Test. Which was of little consolation to the Australians. Down 2-1 in the series, they could no longer take the Ashes from England and at best could hope only to square the rubber at The Oval. This they achieved by five wickets halfway through the sixth day, helped by the absence through injury of Snow, D'Oliveira and Illingworth towards the end.

Lillee put the seal on a remarkable season by taking five wickets in each innings to end the series with 31 wickets, a record for an Australian bowler in England. The two Chappells hit hundreds in Australia's first innings – the first such occurrence by brothers in a Test match while Knott, with a derdoing 92 in the first innings, and newcomer Wood, with a second-innings 90 full of forcing strokes, salvaged England's batting pride. Not one England batsman took a hundred off the Australian bowlers, whereas five were scored by the Australians, two of them by Greg Chappell. Boycott, the one England batsman who might have been expected to do so, missed the last three Tests after Willis, the Warwickshire fast bowler, had split the middle finger of his right hand during a Gillette Cup match.

For their tour of India and Pakistan later in the year, England, or rather MCC, turned to an uncapped player, Lewis, to lead the party and chose as his deputy Denness, who had previously played one Test. Also included was Fletcher, whose one Test of the summer had been at Headingley, where he made such an unhappy début against the 1968 Australians, missing catches and failing to score in his first Test innings. He had done only marginally better against Chappell's side, and it was generally reckoned that the tour was his final chance to establish his England credentials. He proved his class with a sound 97 not out in Madras and a maiden Test

hundred in Bombay, where Greig also scored his first hundred for England. These two were by far the outstanding English batsmen in India, each in his own way coping with India's sleightful spin bowlers. Chandrasekhar, with his whipped-through top-spinners and googlies, finished the five-Test series with 35 wickets; Bedi, in his classical left-arm manner, claimed 25.

Yet in the first Test, at New Delhi, England stunned the whole of India with a victory by six wickets. And this despite Chandra's eight for 79 in their first innings. Needing 207 to win, England were seen home by Lewis with an unbeaten 70, his only innings of substance in the series apart from a glorious attacking century in the fourth Test. By then, however, India had secured a 2-1 lead, winning an exciting match by 28 runs at Calcutta and by four wickets at Madras. Both the fourth and fifth Tests were drawn, Viswanath thwarting England at Kanpur with a rearguard 75 not out and enjoying a hundred, along with Engineer, Greig and Fletcher, at Bombay.

Drawn matches were standard fare when England went north to Pakistan, where Amiss hit 112 at Lahore, 158 in Hyderabad and 99 in Karachi. Hundreds for Pakistan by Asif Iqbal, Mushtaq and Sadiq Mohammad, and Intikhab Alam testified more to the placidness of the pitches than to the quality of the England bowlers at the end of an exhausting tour. The political situation in Pakistan continued to cause concern, and more than an hour and a half of the final Test was lost because of riots and crowd invasions of the pitch. However, it was a duststorm that effected the abandonment of this match 45 minutes before the scheduled close.

Earlier in the season, Pakistan had embarked on an ill-balanced tour of Australia and New Zealand. Given insufficient time to acclimatise, they came up against a confident Australian side full of runs and possessing a strongly built 'tangle-footed' fast-medium swing bowler called Max Walker. In the last Test, at Sydney, he took six for 15 from 16 overs as Australia won for the third time in a row. But disturbing for Australia, as they prepared for a major tour of the West Indies, was the back injury suffered by Lillee in this final victory. Such was his competitiveness, though, that he continued to bowl splendidly at reduced pace in support of Walker.

Worrying in another respect was the

notoriety Lillee had gained after an exchange with the former Pakistan captain, Saeed Ahmed, during the second Test, and the barrage of bumpers he had let fly at Pakistan's lower-order batsmen in the same match. In New Zealand, Pakistan enjoyed their first overseas victory in a series by winning the second Test by an innings and 166 runs, Mushtaq hitting a double-century and taking seven wickets in the match with his leg-spin. The first and third Tests were drawn.

Australia's tour of the West Indies included five Tests. They won the third by 44 runs – after West Indies, chasing 334, were 268 for four at lunch on the last day; and the fourth by 10 wickets. The other three were drawn. When Lillee, out of form in the first Test, broke down in his next match of the tour, in Antigua, and with Massie handicapped by illness and unsympathetic conditions, the bowling was carried by the inexhaustible Walker and Hammond, whose advance and extra yard of pace compensated for the loss of Lillee. Walters, too, made strategic contributions with his medium-pace, and his return to batting form after two troubled series against England strengthened Australia's middle order. The Chappells, Edwards and the obdurate Redpath batted in such a way as to suggest that Ian Chappell had the nucleus of a team which would be very difficult to beat, especially if Lillee could be nursed back to fitness.

West Indies, on the other hand, desperately needed fast bowlers to support their principal wicket-taker, off-spinner Lance Gibbs. In several Tests, Lloyd, at medium-pace, shared the new ball with Boyce, simply to remove the shine for the spinners. It was a far cry from the 1960s when Hall and Griffith instilled fear into batsmen with their speed. Sobers, captain until this series, did not play in any of the Tests as he was recovering from a cartilage operation. His presence, as a player if not necessarily as captain, was sorely missed.

But the real difference between the two teams was attitude, not personal ability. The Australians, to a man, were behind Ian Chappell; Kanhai, the new captain, was bedevilled by the inter-island rivalries that were a recurring problem for West Indian cricket. It was obvious that he would need all his experience and diplomacy if he was to lead a happy and successful team in England in 1973.

Lillee quickly established that he was the fastest bowler on either side. Here, Boycott is discomforted by a well directed bouncer.

Stackpole lived up to his reputation as a lucky batsman being dropped off successive balls from Arnold; here Snow at slip drops the second.

No mistake with Stackpole in the second innings as Greig uproots his leg stump (*above*). Marsh was Australia's top scorer in the match. He cuts D'Oliveira for 4 (*below*), Greig and Luckhurst set off in fruitless pursuit.

Knott falls to a combination that was to become one of the most likely ways of being out (*overleaf*) – caught Marsh bowled Lillee. ▶

Greg Chappell returns to a standing ovation. His 131 was a superb demonstration of technique and was his first Test century in England.

Bob Massie (*above*) took 16 wickets in the match – eight in each innings. Among the victims of his swing bowling were Boycott (*top left*) and Smith (*centre left*). Bruce Francis offers congratulations (*left*) as Chappell, Lillee, Gleeson and Edwards escort him off the field. Massie's performance in his first Test remains the best ever at Lord's and his Test figures the third best of all time.

England's second innings draws to its woeful conclusion; the scoreboard tells the tale at the instant the eighth wicket falls – Snow caught Marsh bowled Massie. Spectators watch in mounting disbelief.

Parfitt takes a splendid catch to dismiss Massie off Snow. Luckhurst is the other slip and Knott the wicket-keeper.

Dennis Lillee in full flow, hair and moustache prominent. D'Oliveira (*right*) looks pensive, perhaps contemplating the next delivery.

Ross Edwards driving during his 170 not out in the second innings. It was only his second Test match, having made his debut at Lord's.

Derek Underwood was recalled for his first Test of the series – a happy choice for England. As it turned out the wicket affected by flooding and a lack of grass was tailor-made for him. He took 10 wickets in the match and three of his six second innings victims are seen opposite. All eyes are on Parfitt (*top*) as he snaps up Walters for 3. Soon after Marsh had a swing and Knott gratefully accepted the thin edge (*centre*). Inverarity was out next ball (*bottom*), Illingworth taking the catch at silly point. England won the match by nine wickets. It is now generally felt, particularly in Australia, that the damage was caused by Fusarium fungus, a grass disease that occurs in damp conditions. Whatever the cause, the spinners took 22 of the 31 wickets to fall.

Greg Chappell catches D'Oliveira off Mallett (*left*). It was D'Oliveira's last Test match.

Greg Chappell reaches his 100 (*below*), his brother Ian at the far end applauds. He also scored 100 in the same innings (*right*), their partnership being worth 201.

Rohan Kanhai during his 105 (*left*) at the picturesque Kensington Oval in Barbados. Max Walker (*below*) was the mainstay of the Australian bowling following Lillee's back injury, which was to keep him out of Test cricket for nearly two years. Greg Chappell (*bottom*) made 100 in the first innings. Lillee (*above*) watches the pre-match practice.

The turning point, which led to an Australian victory ; Marsh catches Kallicharran off Walker (*right*) off the first ball after lunch on the final day. The West Indies innings then collapsed, giving Australia a 44 run victory. Lawrence Rowe suffered an ankle injury (*below*) which resulted in his missing the 1973 tour of England.

A transistor radio — the ear-plug for this one has been lost long ago — is part of nearly every spectator's equipment (*above*).

Stackpole, injured while fielding close, is led back to the pavilion.

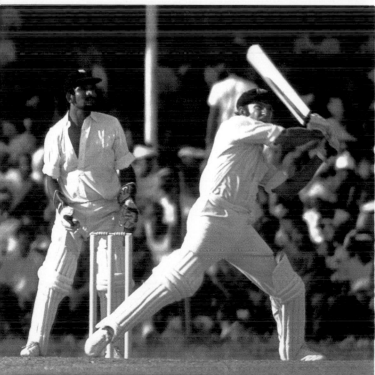

The Australian victory was due in part to a remarkable innings by Doug Walters in which he scored a century between lunch and tea on the first day; at left, he despatches Inshan Ali to the boundary. With Ross Edwards (*above*) he returns to warm applause.

1973/74

1st Test **England v. New Zealand** *Trent Bridge*
2nd Test **England v. New Zealand** *Lord's*
3rd Test **England v. New Zealand** *Headingley*

1st Test **England v. West Indies** *The Oval*
2nd Test **England v. West Indies** *Edgbaston*
3rd Test **England v. West Indies** *Lord's*

Having been dealt such foul hands by the English weather on two previous tours – coffee was served on the field at Edgbaston in 1965 – the New Zealanders of 1973 could be forgiven for viewing with wonderment the warm, sunny days in which they began their tour at Eastbourne. Sleeveless sweaters were much in evidence, and their captain, Bevan Congdon, soon bared his arms to the late April sunshine. Lean and craggy, of granite jaw that would sustain a Snow bouncer when he was 24 in his marathon innings of 176 in the Trent Bridge Test, he was to emerge from the three-match series with the admiration of all.

But, first, the focus of attention was on the New Zealand opening batsman, Turner. With hundreds at Eastbourne, Worcester and Lord's (v MCC), he was well set for 1,000 runs before the end of May (a feat last achieved in 1938 by Sir Donald Bradman and Bill Edrich), although it was not until the last day of the month, at Northampton, that he joined Bradman as the only overseas batsman to complete 1,000 runs before June. In the next match, the New Zealanders' last before the first Test, Turner was dismissed without scoring for the first time on the tour, and it presaged ill: in the Tests he totalled just 116 runs, of which 81 were in his final innings. Ironically, on his return to county cricket, he scored 1,036 runs for Worcestershire, finishing as the season's outstanding batsman with 2,416 runs.

The series, overall, reflected England's professionalism and New Zealand's inexperience. Illingworth, cannily utilising what would soon be revealed as limited resources, campaigned from a defensive position; Congdon, reserved with depths of inner reserves, lacked the judgment, or confidence, to press home winning advantages. His seam bowlers discomforted England's batsmen, with Dayle Hadlee uncovering their disinclination for the rising ball which the West Indians, Holder and Boyce, would exploit later in the season. But in Snow, Arnold, Greig and Old, Illingworth held the stronger hand in favourable conditions, as at Trent Bridge and Headingley. He himself bowled sparingly, and tellingly no New Zealander fell to spin.

At Trent Bridge New Zealand indulged in extremes, bundled out for 97 in their first innings with extras top-scorer at 20. Nor was England's scorecard free of peculiarities. Amiss (138 not out), Greig (139), Arnold (10 not out) and extras were the only second-innings entries in double figures. Then came Congdon's monumental fight-back, supported principally by Pollard (116), which took New Zealand to within 38 runs of victory. Their total of 440 was the second-highest scored in the fourth innings of any Test; and at Lord's a fortnight later their 551 for nine was New Zealand's highest innings in Test cricket. Pollard again reached three figures, as did Burgess, and Congdon confirmed his weakness in negotiating the 170s, falling this time for 175.

Fletcher, with a studious, accomplished 178, saved England from the embarrassment of a first defeat by New Zealand, but Wadsworth's failure to catch Arnold, late in the day, may have been the real turning-point. Fletcher gave further evidence of his maturity by heading the England batting against West Indies, provoking one leading commentator to declare that only he and Greig 'could look forward to the tour in the West Indies without reason to fear that their security would be undermined by the bouncer'. His fielding in Test matches, however, did nowt to temper Yorkshire wit.

Yorkshiremen, nevertheless, had much to savour in the performances at Headingley of their own favourites. Boycott's 115 against New Zealand provided him with a hundred against all the Test-playing countries, and Old, in his first home series, took six wickets. But it was Arnold, with seam and swing, who ripped the heart from the dispirited Kiwis as they slumped to an innings defeat.

Elsewhere, the West Indians were preparing for their mini-series, already capturing the public imagination by their ebullience and multiple talents; formidable assets now welded by the discipline of Kanhai, who was retaining the captaincy even though Sobers was restored to fitness and enthusiasm. Psychologically, they had to overcome the winter's defeats by Australia, but for many, contracted to English counties, the conditions were familiar and often favourable. Moreover, any Test team that could bat at No. 8 Bernard Julien, whose 52 for Kent at Northampton in June required only 12 scoring strokes, and Boyce at No. 9 need not worry unduly about any early-order collapse.

So it proved. At Edgbaston, in the drawn second Test, with Headley, Kanhai, Lloyd, Kallicharran and Sobers dismissed, they recovered from 128 for five to 327. At Lord's, where Sobers, in his farewell Test in England, took leave of his crease after Friday luncheon with 132 and a stomach upset, West Indies' sixth, seventh and eighth wickets put on 313 runs. With the dismissal of Julien for a maiden hundred, off 127 deliveries, and the score recording 604 for seven, what less incentive was there for the flayed England bowlers than the sight of a refreshed Sobers strolling into the sunshine through that little gate in front of the pavilion? Especially when the scoreboard, instead of that customary digit, greeted him with three figures.

Kanhai called it off at 652 for eight, the fourth highest total in *any* match at Lord's, and England went weary to bed at 88 for three, one of them Boycott, attempting to hook a rising ball outside off stump. What hopes fluttered in English hearts fell late next morning when, off successive balls from Gibbs, Sobers at close backward-short-leg snapped up Fletcher and Illingworth. Sobers, absolved of the cares of captaincy, reviewed in this series many of his glories, and none more so than his brilliance close to the bat. His six catches at Lord's equalled the record in a match for a fieldsman other than a wicket-keeper.

The arrival of Willis to join Arnold prolonged the England innings by 90 minutes or more when a bomb hoax brought a request that the ground be cleared. Many spectators ignored it, including an ageing gentleman who had spent the day witnessing the demise of all he held dear. What difference could a bomb make? The West Indians retired to Maida Vale for the offerings from Newmarket and Goodwood; the England players took refuge in a tent behind the pavilion and placed their trust in Lord Harris's influence with the Almighty. He saved them this time, but once play resumed he returned his attentions to Folkestone, where they were equally needed. England followed on before Saturday was out and on Bank Holiday Monday were beaten by an innings and 226 runs. The message was not lost in the halls of hallows. Illingworth, the most professional of professionals, was cast aside and Denness of Kent, albeit a Scot, was installed for the forthcoming tour. Lewis, for whom Denness was deputy in India and Pakistan, could not be considered, having missed most of the season through injury.

Few English reputations had survived without blemish. Hayes, fair of hair and full of firm strokes, aroused expectations with a maiden hundred in the second innings of his first Test, at The Oval, where West Indies, before an enthusiastic 'home crowd', won by 158 runs; but thereafter his contribution was negligible, recalling another débutant hero at The Oval only a year earlier. Wood, also from Lancashire, had since shuffled out of contention on the sub-continent. Hayes would similarly disappear while abroad. Missing from the tour party was Snow, regarded by many as England's finest strike bowler. His omission, said Trevor Bailey, 'could not have been on his ability as a bowler'.

Such a considered opinion, hinting that all was not well within the game, could also find expression in other areas. The conduct of players, a growing cause for concern, was brought into focus at Edgbaston, where Kanhai's open dissent at umpire Fagg's refusal of an appeal for caught behind against Boycott led to Fagg's reluctance to stand again in the match. Reason prevailed, for the moment. But with the increased incidence of 'gamesmanship' commensurable with the higher rewards for victory, plus the instant analysis of the television replay, the pressure on umpires was becoming intolerable for some. Umpires did, however, still find it within their powers to limit the number of short-pitched deliveries, Boyce being cautioned at Lord's for intimidatory bowling.

The behaviour of spectators, too, was not beyond reproach. At Swansea, where England beat New Zealand in a Prudential Trophy match, a hundred by Amiss was greeted by an invasion of the playing area by a young mob intent on applause by assault. At Lord's on the Saturday of the bomb scare, Boycott was jostled by the crowd – some jubilant, some indignant – after hooking the last ball of the day into the safe hands of Kallicharran, specially positioned at long leg. To accommodate the numbers wishing to see the West Indians – and so enrich the coffers – the ground authorities had allowed spectators to sit on the grass, despite the frequency of ground invasions at The Oval. By Monday the crowds had been driven back beyond the pickets, but it was too late. A tradition, nurtured by television, had been established.

Crowd scenes, of a more sinister nature, featured prominently in Denness's first Test as England captain, in volatile Trinidad, in February. When the competitive Greig threw down Kallicharran's wicket at the close of play, umpire Sang Hue, taken by surprise, gave him out; but later in the evening, with the England players besieged in their dressing-room, the appeal was diplomatically withdrawn and Kallicharran continued next day to 158. Photographic record of the incident is limited to an ITN news film, the 'still' photographers having long rushed off to satisfy the early editions, but West Indies' seven-wickets victory is well documented.

The next three Tests were drawn, England being saved from defeat at Kingston by Amiss's unbeaten 262 and by Fletcher's diligent 129 not out at Bridgetown, where the hapless Rowe announced his return with a triple-hundred and where a record 99 no-balls were bowled. Rain prevailed over the Georgetown Test, whereupon the series was squared at Port of Spain. Greig, with his new style off-breaks, won the match for England with match figures of 13 for 156, including a first-innings haul of eight. Boycott was England's other hero with 99 and 112, but by and large he had been overshadowed by Amiss, whose 663 runs in the series included three hundreds. Greig was the star turn throughout, always the extrovert but no off-spinner. If his success convinced him that he was, or England that their days of angst were behind them, the delusion was roughly equal.

Down Under, Australia and New Zealand came together for the first time since March 1946, playing three Tests each in their respective countries. Australia won at home 2-0, while the series in New Zealand was drawn 1-1, hundreds in each innings by Turner and the fast-bowling of the brothers Hadlee propelling New Zealand to their first win over Australia. In the drawn first Test, the Chappells had dominated affairs with a unique fraternal feat, Ian scoring 145 and 121 and Greg 247 not out and 133. There was still no Dennis Lillee, though there was talk of his returning as a batsman and spin bowler. In Sydney, in a late-season state match, another young fast bowler returned from injury to wreck Queensland's first innings with figures of seven for 85. J. R. Thomson, it seemed, had forgotten his previous season's Test début of no wicket for 110 against Pakistan.

ENGLAND	total	2 1 3	for	4
GREIG	1 2 6		extras	9
AMISS	6 5		overs	6 8
			last man FLETCHER	8

bowler	11	10	8	9	3
overs	17	13	16	13	9
wickets	1		1	1	
runs	26	50	49	51	28

	1	2	2	8 3	11	4	2 4 5
6		7		8		9	

	1st inns	2nd inns	umpires	pts
ENGLAND	250		RHODES	
N ZEALAND	97		CONSTANT	
fielder	1 2 3 4 5 6 7 8 9 10 11 S			

The new scoreboard at Trent Bridge during Amiss and Greig's stand.

Congdon was hit on the jaw by this bouncer from Snow (*left*) ; he showed little ill effect, going on to score 176. Turner (*above*) is caught by Roope off Arnold, an anticlimax after he had scored 1000 first class runs before the end of May.

Congdon continued where he left off at Trent Bridge, making 175 (*above, left*). Keith Fletcher saved England from defeat with a solid 178 (*above right*). The moment at which New Zealand failed to win the test was probably the instant (*below*) as Wadsworth drops Arnold off his second ball. Arnold went on to share in a partnership with Fletcher of 92.

Boycott (*above*) made a century in front of his home crowd and helped set up the innings victory.

Probably suffering from a sense of anticlimax after two close Tests, the New Zealand batting collapsed to Snow and Arnold. Here, Parker is caught Knott bowled Arnold for the second time in the match.

Kallicharran (*above*, hooking Snow for 4), made 80 in each innings and contributed to a good all round performance by West Indies who won their first Test match for four years. The most heartening performance for England was Frank Hayes' maiden Test century (*right*).

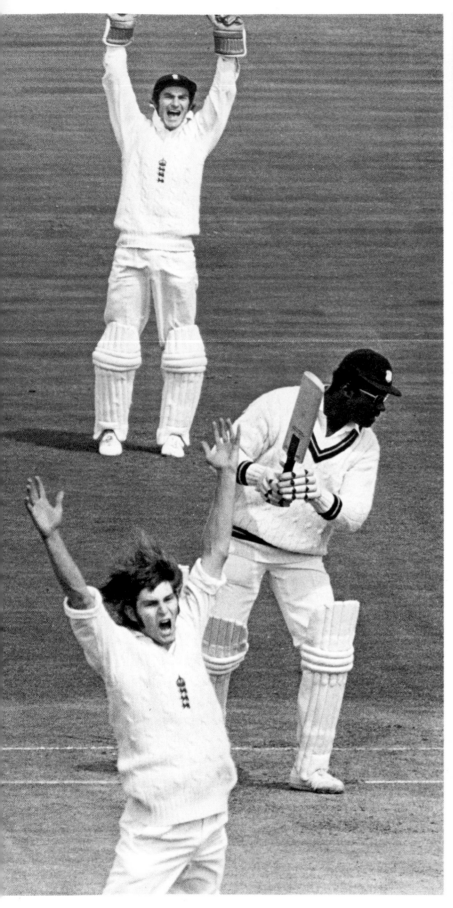

Lloyd falls to Old, lbw (*above*). Fredericks, who made 150, just manages to get back in time to avoid being stumped by Knott off Illingworth (*right*). Kallicharran is at the far end.

Boycott had an up and down sort of match. The West Indies did not agree with umpire Fagg's decision that Boycott had not edged a catch to Murray (*top*); Boycott collided with Murray and suffered a bruised rib (*centre*) which resulted in him retiring hurt. He then resumed, to be hit by Holder and retired hurt again. Meanwhile Alan Oakman had to deputize for Fagg who was so upset by the West Indies reactions that he refused to umpire on the third day.

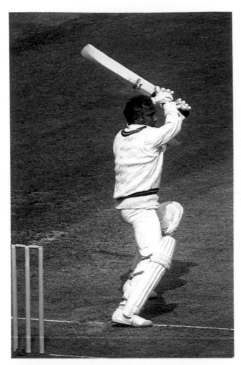

In a crushing victory for the West Indies Kanhai sets the pace with a solid 157.

Gary Sobers in his last Test match in England during his 150 not out.

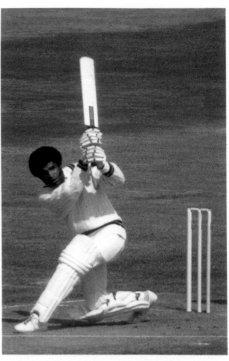

Bernard Julien scores his maiden Test century and helps West Indies to 652.

Julien bowls to Underwood towards the end of England's second innings. All 11 West Indian players appear in the same photograph as England head for a defeat by an innings and 226 runs, their largest ever at the hands of the West Indies. Only Fletcher at the far end put up any resistance, with 86 not out.

Gary Sobers (*right,* during the second Test at Edgbaston), made his 26th and last century during the Lord's Test. This was his last Test match in England and grateful fans say goodbye to the world's greatest all-rounder (*next page*).

1974/75

1st Test **England v. India** *Old Trafford*
2nd Test **England v. India** *Lord's*
3rd Test **England v. India** *Edgbaston*

1st Test **England v. Pakistan** *Headingley*
2nd Test **England v. Pakistan** *Lord's*
3rd Test **England v. Pakistan** *The Oval*

2nd Test **Australia v. England** *Perth*
3rd Test **Australia v. England** *Melbourne*
4th Test **Australia v. England** *Sydney*

Having salvaged honour in the West Indies, England faced another twin series at home, first against an inept India and then against a better-balanced Pakistan who disturbed Denness's men without defeating them. Over the six-Test summer, England called on merely 13 players, of whom Boycott played in only the first Test against India and was replaced by David Lloyd. Edrich, recalled to provide a left-handed counter to the Indian spinners, would end the summer as Denness's deputy for the tour to Australia in defence of the Ashes. He was one of nine over 30 in England's touring party, and nothing that had happened during the season had prepared any of them for what lay in store.

India's bowling strength was once more their quartet of spin, but Bedi, Chandrasekhar, Prasanna and Venkataraghavan were thwarted jointly by atrocious weather early on the tour and the ability – even willingness – of the England batsmen to go down the wicket to them. While spin accounted for 15 of the 24 England wickets that fell in the three Tests, it was expensive: each wicket cost 67.46 runs. In the second Test, which England won by an innings and 285 runs, Bedi (six for 226 from 64.2 overs) became the first bowler to concede 200 runs in a Test at Lord's;

at Edgbaston, England lost only two wickets in winning the third Test by an innings and 78 runs.

Amiss topped the England aggregate for the series with 370 runs, Lloyd, Fletcher and Edrich averaged over 100, and Denness helped himself to successive hundreds. Such free-scoring made Boycott's difficulties with India's gentle medium-pace bowlers all the more surprising. Omitted from the side after the first Test to help him sort out his problems in county matches, he was chosen for Australia but inexplicably withdrew to self-imposed isolation.

Only at Manchester, where wind, hail and rain were a travesty of cricketing conditions and a TV crew refused to work on their tower unless adequate shelter was provided, did India approach a winning position. An enterprising declaration by Denness gave them the final day to score 296, but in the last hour, their batsmen having been uncertain whether to chase victory or avoid defeat, they were beaten by 113 runs. Old returned figures of four for 20 and improved on them with five for 21 at Lord's, where he and Arnold (four for 19) exploited the heavy cloud-cover and the eagerness of the Indian batsmen to self-destruct.

It was seam, however, not speed that routed the Indians repeatedly, and in

the second half of the summer Pakistan's batsmen, many of them county players, put the England bowling in truer perspective. Similarly, their own varied attack showed England's batting in more honest light. Only on the plumbest of Oval wickets were there hundreds. Amiss, with 183, took his Test runs in a calendar year to 1,253; Fletcher's slow century was a less enviable achievement. Zaheer's 240 at The Oval was the only three-figure score recorded by Pakistan in the series.

Once again the weather was a decisive factor, ensuring that the first two Tests were drawn; as was the third. Not even the new regulation, allowing play to continue until 7.30 should an hour or more be lost, could overcome the whims of the heavens. At Headingley, the last day was washed out with England, having fought tenaciously to overcome a first-innings deficit, 238 for six overnight and needing another 44 runs to win. Arnold, with his late movement, was England's most dangerous bowler, benefiting from the cloudy conditions and the uneven bounce of a slowish wicket.

At Lord's, too, weather and wicket were critical, though in more controversial circumstances. A sunny first morning was shattered by a violent storm which broke as Pakistan's openers were capitalising on first use of a beautiful batting track. The playing conditions of the time being explicit on such matters, the pitch remained uncovered: when Pakistan resumed five hours later they went from 51 without loss to 130 for nine declared. Underwood, in his element, took as many wickets (five) as in his four previous Tests; and was to be presented with eight more in the second innings when 'an appalling show of negligence and incompetence' allowed the heavy rain of Sunday and Monday morning to seep under the covers and soak the pitch. Poor Pakistan had already retrieved their position once. Their bowlers had England 118 for six in their first innings before Knott's puckish 83 saw them to 270, and by close of play on Saturday their batsmen had put them 33 runs ahead with seven wickets in hand. When, at 5.15 on Monday evening, play got under way, Underwood cut down the remaining Pakistan batsmen. In 11.5 overs he took six wickets for nine runs and left England wanting 87 runs for victory. However, the authorities were saved from further embarrassment when Tuesday brought further rain and the umpires, perhaps percipiently, abandoned the match at 4.30.

India, by this time, had returned home to a committee of enquiry into their poor performance. Wadekar, their captain, retired from first-class cricket, at 33, and the Nawab of Pataudi was recalled to lead his country against the West Indies side touring India, Sri Lanka and Pakistan under Clive Lloyd. As he showed with an average of 79.50 in the five Tests against India, Lloyd did not allow his belligerent batting to suffer from his new responsibilities.

West Indies won three Tests, the first by 267 runs with decisive contributions from two Hampshire players: Gordon Greenidge, on his début, opened with 93 and 107 and Roberts took three wickets in each innings, matching the quickest of the current fast bowlers for speed and ferocity. I. V. A. Richards, another débutant, was less successful but made amends with an unbeaten 192 in the second Test, which India lost by an innings. But then the Indians came back strongly to win the next two Tests, so restoring national pride, and with the series squared the final Test at Bombay was extended to six days. Lloyd put his side in a winning position with a marvellous 242 not out, unwittingly precipitating a near riot when the crowd reacted strongly to police handling of a

spectator who came out to congratulate Lloyd on his double-hundred. There was crowd trouble in Pakistan, too, the two and a half hours lost on the second day at Karachi probably preventing West Indies from forcing a victory which would have given them the two-Test series. All Lloyd's side performed well, and it did not pass without notice that it had been on a tour of India and Pakistan in 1958-59 that the great West Indies side of the 1960s first showed its potential.

England, battered and bruised in Australia, could not face the future with similar optimism. Their opponents, on the other hand, could. Lillee, despite reports to the contrary, was found to be fit and bowling faster with every outing. To support him was Thomson who, through sheer strength and pace, made the ball lift alarmingly from just short of a length to temple height. They were first encountered in Brisbane, on a pitch of uneven bounce hastily prepared by Alderman Clem Jones, the mayor, following severe flooding. Amiss had a thumb broken by Thomson, Edrich had his hand broken by Lillee. Only Greig, helped by his height and an oft-employed slash over the arc of slips, had the wherewithal to counter, scoring the only hundred of the match.

England's dearth of young talent was amply illustrated by the arrival in Perth of Colin Cowdrey, two weeks short of his 43rd birthday, to cover for Amiss and Edrich. Immediately, he was pitched into the arena, bravely scoring 22 and 41 as Australia won by nine wickets and went two up in the series. Thomson took his Test tally to 16, Lillee bagged another four, and the pattern was set: explosive fast bowling supported by a brilliance in the field that at times was breathtaking. At Perth, slips and gully shared 13 catches. Greg Chappell's seven for the match were a record for a non-wicket-keeper.

Furthermore, Australia's batting was coming into its own, Walters treating England's bowlers with such disdain at Perth that he could reach a century between tea and the close with a six off Willis, England's fastest bowler. He returned to a standing ovation from the crowd and a dressing-room devoid of team-mates – until a head popped from behind a shower-stall to ask 'How did it go, Doug?' Next morning Ross Edwards also reached three figures, and although Redpath, in the fourth Test, and Greg Chappell, in the fourth and sixth, were the Australians' only other

century-makers, their batting had a consistency that England's could not match. Led aggressively by Ian Chappell, Australia were a cock-a-hoop outfit, if too cocksure for English observers.

Just how influential Thomson's presence was is best illustrated by his absence. At Adelaide, in the fifth Test, having taken his Test wickets to 33, he sprained his right shoulder playing tennis on the rest day and took no further part in the series. In England's second innings Knott, who had already proved the virtues of getting into line, hit only the second hundred by a wicket-keeper in Anglo-Australian Tests. By then, however, Lillee and the admirable Walker had ensured Australia's fourth victory by destroying the early order. At Melbourne, where Lillee bowled only six overs, England won the sixth Test by an innings with Denness, who had dropped himself for the fourth Test, scoring 188 and Fletcher 146. On the first morning Peter Lever had put Australia under pressure with a spell of four for five in six overs.

There were further, successive, hundreds for Denness (181) and Fletcher (216) at Auckland in the first of two Tests against New Zealand. But, ironically in view of what they had experienced in Australia, England's innings victory at Auckland was marred by the near-tragic accident to the New Zealand No. 11 batsman, Ewan Chatfield. Deflecting a bouncer from Lever on to his temple, he collapsed, his heart stopped beating, and only prompt action by Bernard Thomas, the MCC physiotherapist, and a St John's Ambulanceman saved him.

England had left Australian cricket riding on the crest of a wave. The dual prospect of seeing Lillee and Thomson in tandem and of watching 'the poms being stuffed' attracted huge crowds. The drawn third Test at Melbourne, where Australia finished eight runs short of victory with two wickets in hand, drew more than a quarter of a million spectators; and at Sydney, where Australia regained the Ashes, the attendance of 178,027 was a record for the SCG. With receipts high, the game was prosperous – yet the players making it so were receiving just $200 a Test. With tail-enders as well as specialist batsmen putting their life on the line against the rising use of the short-pitched delivery, such remuneration in an inflationary and materialistic age fell well short of some expectations. The seeds of discontent were germinating.

Defeat for India as Knott stumps Chandrasekhar off Greig (*above left*). Edrich and Denness join in the appeal.

Gavaskar (*above right*) hooks during his first innings century.

Farewell to Boycott (*left*) as he falls lbw to the medium pace of Abid Ali in England's first innings. This was to be his last Test for over three years.

Viswanath (*right*) is bowled by Underwood ; all players are suitably sweatered for one of the coldest Test matches in living memory.

Dennis Amiss (*top*) was England's top scorer with 188. Greig and Denness also made centuries in England's score of 629.

Rival wicket-keepers on collision course (*facing page*) as Engineer scrambles home and Knott, to his credit, stands his ground. India's second innings collapse was sudden and total ; Arnold and Old, being photographed celebrating by colleague Eric Piper (*right*), finished them off in an hour and a quarter for 42, the lowest ever Test score at Lord's. Viswanath (*left*) is caught by Knott off Arnold.

A high speed sequence of B.S. Bedi; he toiled and spun in vain during this Test, taking only one of the two English wickets to fall.

David Lloyd during his 214 not out. For the second successive Test match India lost by an innings.

Majid Khan (*left*) during his 75, the top score of the match. Wasim Bari catches Lloyd off Sarfraz (*top*) and Sarfraz enjoys a leg side 4 during his half century. The match ended in a rainy draw.

Sadiq Mohammad (*above*), with the apparently headless Lloyd at short leg, started well with Majid Khan until rain soaked the wicket (*below left*). Underwood was in his element in the resulting conditions (*below right*) and took five for 20 in the first innings.

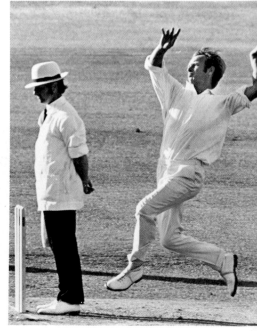

Pakistan had little more luck in the second innings when rain soaked under the covers. Wasim Raja is caught Lloyd off Underwood (*above*) and Intikhab Alam is bowled by Underwood (*below*). Underwood finished with second innings figures of eight for 51. Rain prevented play and a certain English victory on the last day. This was just as well as the Pakistanis were unhappy with the Lord's rain-proofing.

Zaheer Abbas made 240. His first century came from this edge through the slips off Old (*far left*), and his double century was greeted by fellow country-men and one member of the Kennington police force (*above*) A hardly recognisable Derek Underwood stayed too long as night-watchman and had to demonstrate his technique against the short pitched delivery (*left*). Dennis Amiss (*below*) showed his liking for conditions at the Oval with 183, while Fletcher had the doubtful distinction of scoring the slowest first class century in England. Needless to say the match ended as a draw.

Walters (*above*) scored a century in the final session of the second day's play. Earlier a jet-lagged and winter-pale Cowdrey had experienced at first hand what he had watched on television just two weeks before – an express bouncer barrage from Lillee (*centre*) and Thomson. In the second innings he opens the England innings with David Lloyd (*right*).

In Jeff Thomson (*above*), Australia found the perfect partner for Dennis Lillee. His delivery was unconventional, resembling a javelin throw with his slinging action. Cowdrey remarked that the ball disappeared behind Thomson's body, only reappearing at the last moment, just before delivery – making him doubly difficult to play.

Knott (*top right*) – being caught by Marsh – and Titmus (*bottom right*) – after a painful blow on the knee – would agree. The remainder of the English batsmen, battered, bruised or dismissed would feel the same way.

David Lloyd (*left*) starts the long walk back to the dressing room having become a victim of both fast bowlers simultaneously – caught Thomson bowled Lillee. Keith Fletcher takes evasive action (*top*) as a ball from Thomson passes at temple height. The Doug

Walters Stand, alias The Sydney Hill, was packed for all five days of the match – it was a record crowd as New South Wales flocked to watch Australia regain the Ashes.

Ian Redpath (105) and Greg Chappell (144) (*top left*) enabled Australia to set England a target of 400 for victory. Apart from Greig (*left*), who made 54 before being stumped by Marsh off Mallett (*far left*) England were unable to cope with the combined force of Lillee, Thomson, Walker and Mallett. Australia won by 171 runs and regained the Ashes lost to Illingworth's side four years beforehand, on the same ground.

1975/76

1st Test **England v. Australia** *Edgbaston*
2nd Test **England v. Australia** *Lord's*
3rd Test **England v. Australia** *Headingley*
4th Test **England v. Australia** *The Oval*

1st Test **Australia v. West Indies** *Brisbane*
2nd Test **Australia v. West Indies** *Perth*
3rd Test **Australia v. West Indies** *Melbourne*
4th Test **Australia v. West Indies** *Sydney*

After what had seemed like 18 months of rain, summer returned to England in 1975. With it came Ian Chappell's victorious Australians for a four-Test series that would follow the inaugural World Cup, held throughout June. For cricket lovers, the season promised a feast of entertainment; for England's shell-shocked batsmen there was the daunting prospect of further confrontation with Lillee and Thomson. Geoffrey Boycott, technically England's best batsman, declared himself unavailable for the series and took 1,915 runs (average 73.65) off county bowlers.

Despite a dislike for limited-overs cricket – regarded as an English innovation to rekindle public interest – the Australians bundled England out of the World Cup and shared with West Indies a cliff-hanger of a final that lasted until 8.43 p.m. It was the longest day in cricket history, played fortunately on the longest day of the year: world-wide, televiewing millions were held spellbound as the Australians failed by just 17 runs. Back home, all-night Aussies swanned off to bed on Sunday morning little realising how influential their participation would be on the future of cricket. One of their number had experienced the excitement; now he wanted his share of the audience ratings. Later in the year, Kerry Packer wrote to the Australian Cricket Board to negotiate for exclusive TV rights to first-class cricket for his Channel 9 network, only to be told that these had

been sold to the Australian Broadcasting Commission for much less than he was prepared to pay.

For Chappell's men, the one-day success was a bonus. The tour became serious with the approach of the first Test at Edgbaston and the defence of the Ashes. There was, furthermore, concern over Thomson's inability to adjust to the slow English wickets, and he began the Test series with first-class figures of one for 230 for the tour: in England's first innings, his first two overs produced five wides and he was quickly withdrawn. Walker thus joined Lillee, aggressive, accurate and unplayable, in the dismissal of England for 101 on a rain-affected pitch.

Australia, by the magnanimity of Denness, had already batted. The England captain's decision was incompatible with the nature of the pitch (ideal for batting) or the weather forecast (rain imminent) and it was to cost him and England dear. Australia compiled a sound 359 and were not required to bat a second time. A storm broke over Birmingham after one over of England's first innings; following on they managed 173 only because of Fletcher's 51 and late resistance from Knott and Snow, the latter, at 33, recalled to lead the England attack. Thomson, given the ball when the shine was off, bowled fast and well for five wickets while Lillee and Walker each took his match haul to seven.

The response to England's débâcle

was decisive. Out went Denness, Fletcher, Arnold and Old; in came Wood, Woolmer, David Steele and Peter Lever for the Lord's Test. Greig, England's most combative figure, was given the captaincy, and when the coin fell his way he chose to bat. Little more than an hour later he found himself walking out to join Steele with the score 49 for four. Lillee had accounted for all four batsmen at a personal cost of 27 runs.

John Arlott described Steele, currently enjoying a marvellous summer with unfashionable Northamptonshire, as resembling a bank clerk going to war; certainly his prematurely grey hair and his spectacles belied a speed of reaction that enabled him to compete in workmanlike manner with Australia's fast men. Batting at Number 3, he had scores of 50, 45, 73, 92, 39 and 66 in the series, and at 33 he was England's find of the summer. At Lord's, he stood firm while Greig (96) carried the battle to the Australians. Knott and Woolmer further reflected the new spirit in the England dressing-room, and for the first time England passed 300 against Lillee and Thomson. When, by Friday luncheon, Australia were 64 for six, bright sunshine was not all that warmed the crowds picnicking by the boundary boards.

In the afternoon, Edwards and Thomson averted the follow-on and Lillee, with three sixes and eight fours, gave the innings substance. On Saturday, when for the third successive day the gates were closed on a full house, only two England wickets fell as England patiently consolidated. Edrich scored his seventh hundred against Australia and, when dismissed on Monday, had batted nine hours for his 175. Greig's declaration, giving the Australians 480 minutes to score 484, left neither side much hope for victory on a sluggish wicket.

It was a more confident England side which came together at Headingley for the third Test. A different-looking one, too, with Amiss, Lever, Gooch and Woolmer absent. Hampshire and Old came in on their home ground; so, to the scene of his former torments, did Fletcher to endure further purgatory. Edmonds of Middlesex joined Underwood lest fusarium fungus strike twice. But in the event vandals struck, thinking they might advance their campaign for the release from imprisonment (for armed robbery) of one George Davis by digging holes in the pitch and filling them with sump oil.

Before this, Edmonds had enjoyed his moment of glory, capturing both Chappells and Edwards for four runs on the second afternoon and finishing with five for 28 as Australia were bowled out for 135 in reply to England's 288. Steele's concentration throughout most of Saturday and early Monday provided the backbone of England's second-innings 291, while Gilmour, Australia's first change of the series, revealed Chappell's depth of fast bowling with nine wickets for the match.

When McCosker and Marsh began Australia's chase for 445 – and it was taken up in earnest – the odds were 9-1 against their achieving victory. By close of play they had been halved to 9-2, as had Australia's target for the loss of Marsh and the Chappells. McCosker, 95 overnight, was on the verge of scoring his maiden Test hundred and hopes were high for the England victory that would square the series. Injustice prevailed: the pitch was sabotaged and the match abandoned, although rain at midday would have prevented a result anyway.

Australia had retained the Ashes, and nothing that happened at The Oval would alter that. Not that much could happen on that dreariest of Oval wickets. McCosker scored his well-deserved hundred, Ian Chappell signalled his final Test as Australia's captain with a remorseless 192, and Woolmer, after England had been made to follow on by the inspired bowling of Lillee,

Thomson and Walker, averted ignominy with a slow, sure 149 as England ground on to 538. As a sixth day had been allocated it was, in more ways than one, the longest Test match played in England.

For the England players there now came a much-needed rest. The Australians went home to a six-Test series against West Indies, although in other circumstances they would have been going to South Africa. They had a new captain in Greg Chappell, but Ian still stood alongside him in the slips and, apart from the absence of Walters (injured) and Edwards (retired), they remained 'Chappelli's boys'. The return of Redpath to open the innings strengthened the batting, as evidenced by his hundreds in the third, fifth and sixth Tests.

After two Tests the series stood at one-all. Australia won the first at Brisbane, on another of Alderman Jones's wickets, thanks to a century in each innings by Greg Chappell and some unbelievably indisciplined batting from the West Indians. West Indies burst back at Perth through the inspired batting of Fredericks, whose hundred came off 71 balls, and the hostile pace of Roberts, who took nine wickets. Lloyd, whose tactics as captain were open to question throughout the series, crashed a typical 149, and there was much to admire in the lissome approach of Holding, already faster than Roberts, Thomson and Lillee. He was not fit for Melbourne, where Lillee and Thomson found moisture, movement and the edge of flashing bats on the first day; but why did he never share the new ball with Roberts at Sydney where the West

Ian Chappell, Greg Chappell and Rodney Marsh in conference at Lord's. This was Ian's last series as captain of Australia.

Indians, for their own morale as well as for the series, desperately needed a victory?

In the third Test, on a Melbourne wicket slower than that of Perth, Thomson was fearsomely fast and for the third time in a row the match was over in four days. So was the fourth, again in Australia's favour, and once more it was as much the West Indians' injudicious stroke-play that hastened them to defeat as it was Australia's bowling. Without Lillee, unfit, in support, Thomson reaped six for 50 in West Indies' second-innings slump to 128.

Thereafter, the 'series of the century' was an anti-climax, with Australia winning handsomely in Adelaide and finally at Melbourne. As Roberts' fitness problems reduced his effectiveness, Australia's 'big guns' inflicted the greater damage, and their batsmen always played the more disciplined innings. Indeed, only in the final stages did a West Indian batsman assume the responsibility required in a Test match. Promoted to open the innings, Vivian Richards scored 30 and 101 in the fifth Test and 50 and 98 in the sixth, never forsaking his natural flair but always treating the bowling on its merit. On his return to the islands the 24-year-old Antiguan took 556 runs off the touring Indian bowlers in six innings.

India had gone straight to the Caribbean from a drawn three-Test series in New Zealand. *Wisden* recorded them as leaving the West Indies resembling 'Napoleon's troops on the retreat from Moscow'. Yet in between, Bedi's team had covered themselves in glory, winning the third Test in Trinidad by scoring 406 (for four!) in their second innings. Only once before had a team – the 1948 Australians – achieved victory in such a manner.

In the first Test they had come up against Roberts and Holding, as well as Richards, and had lost by an innings in three days. The second Test was drawn. All, therefore, hung on the fourth and final match at Kingston, and West Indies won in four days. Three Indian batsmen fell in action in the first innings; five were 'absent hurt' in India's second innings. Holding, bowling short-pitched deliveries from round the wicket, so giving the batsmen less time to withdraw from the firing-line, took to an extreme the lessons learnt in Australia. An era, for some time dawning, was breaking into a long day. It was the age of the projectile.

England collapsed on a rain affected pitch after Australia's 359. Here Denness, captaining England for the last time, is caught by Greg Chappell off Walker for 3.

Gooch, playing in his first Test, was caught Marsh bowled Walker for 0 ; he failed to score in the second innings as well.

Greig had made 8 before he too was caught Marsh bowled Walker. England were all out for 101 in the first innings.

▶ Australia won the Test by an innings and collectively congratulate Marsh (*overleaf*) after he had caught Edrich in England's second innings. From left to right Marsh, Walters, I. Chappell, Edwards, Turner, McCosker, Mallett, Walker, G. Chappell and Lillee. Thomson was approaching from the other direction and failed to make the photograph.

Tony Greig, having replaced Denness as captain, shows all his enthusiasm (*top*) after catching Walters off Lever. The Australian tail-end helped Edwards (99) stage a dramatic recovery, Dennis Lillee making 73. A measure of the frustration felt by England can be gauged by the fact that the intrepid John Lever bowled Thomson a bouncer (*right*).

As the Test faded into a tedious draw, the large crowd on a hot fourth day were treated to a display from one Michael Angelow (*top*) Test cricket's first streaker.

John Edrich ensured England's safety with a thoroughly professional 175 (*left*).

Phil Edmonds had a dramatic entry into Test cricket; he dismissed Ian Chappell and Ross Edwards with successive balls, and here delivers the next to Doug Walters. The Test ended when the pitch was damaged by vandals overnight and the match was declared a draw.

Lillee and Greig spent the series in
confrontation (*right*) ; at The Oval Lillee had
the upper hand, dismissing Greig twice, and
hitting him so that he dropped his bat.

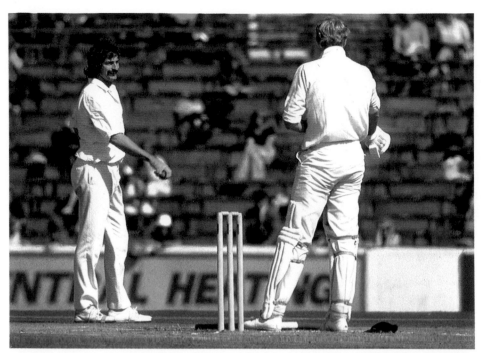

After the experience of Headingley, security precautions were
increased at The Oval; to include floodlighting and an all night dog
patrol (*above*). McCosker made a century in Australia's first innings,
of what turned out to be a protracted draw (*right*).

West Indies went in to lunch on the first day with the score at 125 for six ; victims included Greenidge (*above*), who never really adjusted to Australian conditions on his first visit, here lbw to Lillee for 0 offering no stroke, and Richards (*top right*) brilliantly caught by Gilmour off Lillee also for 0.

Greg Chappell (*right*), in his first Test as Australia's captain, pulls Gibbs for 4. He scored a century in each innings, the second largely through some unselfish batting by his brother Ian.

Ian Redpath (*below*) does not appear to be completely in control after a Roberts bouncer.

Ian Chappell hooks Andy Roberts for 4 during his first innings of 41. He batted well throughout and steered his brother to two centuries and victory.

Lawrence Rowe was the most successful of the West Indian batsmen, making 107.

West Indies won a dramatic Test, largely through the efforts of Fredericks and Roberts. Fredericks (*left*) made an extraordinary 169 hooking and cutting all the Australian bowlers with disdain. In spite of a fighting 156 by Ian Chappell (*top left*), Australia could not match the West Indies innings of 585. With fielding like the Lloyd catch to dismiss Lillee off Julien (*far left*) Australia lost by an innings. Andy Roberts (*above*) took seven for 54 in the second innings.

On the first day (Boxing Day) the second largest crowd ever at the Melbourne Cricket Ground (85,596) came to watch (*far right*). Ian Chappell (*above*) took his 100th catch in Test cricket as Rowe edged a ball from Thomson. Gibbs is seen bowling to Cosier (*right*). Although Cosier stole the headlines with a century in his first Test innings, Gibbs broke Trueman's world record number of Test wickets when the teams returned to Melbourne for the sixth Test of the series in February.

Australia won the series when they scored their third victory. West Indies had an unhappy time, being convinced that Ian Chappell had edged his first ball to Murray. The umpire thought otherwise (*right*). There was no doubt though about this catch by Lloyd to dismiss Walker, in spite of the spectacular dive by Richards (*below*). Australia ruthlessly pursued their advantage after Chappell had been dropped on 11 and had gone on to make an undefeated 182. Marsh dives to catch Rowe off Thomson in the second innings (*far right*). The crowd got through their share of cans in the excitement.

1976/77

1st Test **England v. West Indies** *Trent Bridge*
2nd Test **England v. West Indies** *Lord's*
3rd Test **England v. West Indies** *Old Trafford*
4th Test **England v. West Indies** *Headingley*
5th Test **England v. West Indies** *The Oval*

2nd Test **India v. England** *Calcutta*
3rd Test **India v. England** *Madras*

Centenary Test **Australia v. England** *Melbourne*

At the beginning of the 1970s, cricket in some countries was considered to be in the doldrums. Public interest was on the wane; gate-takings were falling alarmingly. By the middle of the decade, the mood had changed. Such individuals as Lillee, Thomson, the Chappells, Richards and Roberts, had by force of personality or performance stamped their impression on the game, attracting large crowds to see them in action for their countries. But it was *for their countries*, against the stars of other countries, that the cricket spectator wanted to see his heroes play, and cricket's administrators were quick to see the potential of their product. They had a goose, called Test cricket, and they put it in a battery to boost the production of golden eggs. In the period from May 1975 to April 1976, 16 Tests had been played in four series; in the same period the following year there were 26 Tests in seven series, plus the Australia-England Centenary Test. Each eligible country staged Test matches.

West Indies set the egg rolling with a visit to England. And if there were any doubts about their ability to draw multi-racial Britons, Tony Greig, England's South African-bred captain, controversially dispelled them by announcing his intention to make the West Indians 'grovel'. It was not surprising, however disgraceful the scene, that jubilant West Indian supporters flooded on to The Oval pitch when Holding,

having twice been driven gloriously for fours by Greig, bowled him. It was all but the final humiliation for the England captain. On the fifth day Holding, at his fastest, again uprooted Greig's stumps and bowled England out on a featherbed to finish with 14 wickets for the match and settle the series 3-0 in West Indies' favour. The first two Tests were drawn.

Holding's superlative display at The Oval, where Roberts and Willis looked pedestrian by comparison, justified to the last the West Indians' decision to rely almost exclusively on their fast bowlers. Roberts and Holding each took 28 wickets in the series and were well supported by Holder and Daniel. Rarely was there rest for England's beleaguered batsmen – except when Holding and Daniel were strolling back to their marks. An over-rate of 12 to 14 an hour was standard fare for the paying public when West Indies were in the field; and England were not always blameless. Only twice did West Indies play their recognised spinners, and then it was a policy of insurance rather than of tactics. Between them, Jumadeen and Padmore, who shared 117 wickets on the tour, bowled only 31 overs in the Tests. On the other hand, Underwood was England's most successful bowler with 17 wickets, followed by Snow with 15 from three Tests.

The dichotomy in the England camp was that while their batsmen wished for plumb wickets, their bowlers, with the

task of dismissing a line-up of awesome power, wanted anything but. Greenidge and Richards each hit three hundreds, the former one in each innings at Old Trafford plus one at Leeds, and the latter double-hundreds at Trent Bridge and The Oval and 135 at Old Trafford to take his Test runs for the calendar year to 1,710. At Leeds, where Greig and Knott both scored 116 for England, Greenidge and Fredericks launched West Indies' first innings with 50 off eight overs and 100 off 18.2; at the close they were 437 for nine, off only 83 overs. Yet Greig's batting threatened to wrest the game from West Indies until Daniel, on the last day, finished England off and West Indies went two up.

The first Test, at Trent Bridge, had been drawn after a tenacious display by the veterans, Edrich and Close, the latter recalled at 45 after an absence of nine years from Test cricket. The second Test might have gone England's way had not rain washed out all of Saturday's play – one of the few days lost in the hottest summer in living memory. Snow and Underwood had bowled out West Indies 68 in arrears on Friday, but England needed all three days to establish a big lead and dismiss their opponents a second time. Two were not enough, even though Greig kept up the pressure until the last over.

At Old Trafford England were annihilated, dismissed for 71 and 126 and losing by 425 runs. Roberts took nine wickets and three times was on a hat-trick: at the third attempt, having had to wait through an over and a drinks interval before his next delivery, he saw Greenidge at slip put down the all-important catch. Holding, in addition to his seven wickets, collected a warning from umpire Alley for intimidation after bowling three consecutive bouncers at the resolute Close.

Holding, however, was fortunate. In Karachi, in early November, umpire Shuja-ud-Din had Imran Khan withdrawn from the attack after he bowled three consecutive bouncers at Richard Hadlee, New Zealand's Number 8 batsman. The New Zealanders, in order to accommodate the orgy of Test cricket, had travelled to Pakistan before the start of their own domestic season and, after two warm-up games, were playing a Test match in Lahore. For Pakistan, Javed Miandad became the youngest player to score a hundred on début: for New Zealand, off-spinner Petherick, playing in his first Test at 34, performed the hat-trick.

A month later, having lost two Tests and drawn one, the New Zealanders were sweltering in Bombay, losing to India in the first match of a three-Test series, played within the space of 21 days. By the time they were losing the third, having drawn the second, Greig's MCC side was playing its first match in India and the Pakistanis were packing for Australia – or in some cases, unpacking. Because many of Pakistan's leading players had demanded more money for the tour, they were not selected, whereupon the politicians intervened, the original team was disbanded, a new panel of selectors was appointed, and a full-strength touring party was chosen!

In India, Greig's antics both on and off the field raised him almost to the level of a deity in the eyes of the thousands upon enthusiastic thousands who flock inside and outside the stadia there. More importantly, his players responded to him, and for the first time in five tours to India since the Second World War, England won a series. In fact the victory, by three Tests to one, could hardly have been more decisive. Or, for Englishmen, welcome. The fielding was of the highest standard, in the air and on the ground, and the bowling, until the final stages, kept a stranglehold on the Indian stroke-makers. Only Gavaskar took a hundred off the England attack, and that was in the fifth Test, which India won. Willis came of age as a strike bowler, Under-

wood outdid his Indian counterparts for subtlety and accuracy, and John Lever, helped by a 'rogue ball' at New Delhi, took 10 wickets on his début to set England on their winning run. If England's batting was less impressive it mattered less. Bedi had already bowled 200 overs in three weeks of Test cricket against New Zealand and was plainly jaded. So, too, were his cohorts. Amiss and Greig alone hit Test hundreds, while Knott, Brearley, Tolchard and Lever were the only others to score more than 100 runs in the entire series.

At the end of February England moved south, via Sri Lanka, to Australia for the Test match in Melbourne to commemorate 100 years of Test cricket.

Brian Close, seen here on the receiving end of the West Indies bouncer barrage, during the third Test at Old Trafford.

It meant adjusting to new conditions, but they could take heart from the news that Thomson would not be sharing the new ball with Lillee. He had fractured his bowling shoulder in a fielding accident during the first Test against Pakistan. In addition, the Pakistanis had exposed weaknesses in an Australian side without Ian Chappell, Redpath and Mallett, all of whom had retired. Beaten in the second Test at Melbourne by the exemplary fast bowling of Lillee (21 wickets in three Tests), Pakistan came back strongly in Sydney to win by eight wickets and so square the series. Imran, whose speed, hostility and control troubled all the batsmen, took six wickets in each innings.

The Australians then went to New Zealand, where Lillee's 11 wickets won them the second Test and the series, and the Pakistanis endured the long flight to the West Indies – only their second tour there and 18 years after the first. West Indies, without Holding and Daniel, had unearthed two formidable replacements in Croft and the giant Garner, both virtually unknown at the start of the season. Consequently pace again prevailed as they won by two Tests to one, with two drawn, in an exciting and entertaining conflict. Pakistan, too, relied heavily on their fast brigade, although Mushtaq Mohammad, with eight wickets to accompany his 121 and 56 in his side's win at Port of Spain, made a belated plea for the conservation of the leg-spinner.

By now it was April, and England had returned home to await the Australians. They had lost the Centenary Test by 45 runs – magically the same margin as Australia won the first-ever Test – amid a great deal of emotion, euphoria and subterfuge. Lillee, whose 11 wickets in the match had ensured Australia's victory, had announced he would not be touring England: he wanted to rest for the next Australian season. Tony Greig was having a rest, too: in the Caribbean where, in four days, he helped secure the signatures of eight foremost West Indian and Pakistani players to contracts for Mr Kerry Packer. Already 10 Australians, among them Lillee, the Chappells, Marsh, Redpath and Walters, had similar contracts in their pockets, some of them signed during the great celebration at Melbourne. Cricket's revolution, like so many other revolutions, was being put in progress while its leaders wined and dined on the profits engendered by its players.

Tony Greig was the West Indies' prime target after he had proclaimed in a television interview that he intended to make them grovel. Andy Roberts strikes home in the first innings.

Viv Richards (*right*) was unstoppable and reinforced his claim to be the world's best batsman when he scored 232 in West Indies' first innings. The match ended in a draw.

Gordon Greenidge (*left*) falls over while hitting Snow for 6; Brian Close seems unconcerned, but impressed.

David Steele (*right*) steps into his forward defence stroke, as resolute against the West Indies as he had been against Australia.

The match flickered in its dying moments. Greig applies pressure as all 10 England fielders crowd Murray, but the result was a draw.

3rd Test England v. West Indies Old Trafford

▶ Underwood, who always said that he preferred to play at a bouncer rather than attempt to duck it, comes hopelessly and dangerously unstuck against this one from Holding (*overleaf*). The English batsmen, notably Close and Edrich, faced more than their fair share of short pitched deliveries. They managed only 71 and 126 and were beaten by an innings and 425 runs. Greenidge made a century in each innings for the West Indies, comfortably outscoring England on his own account.

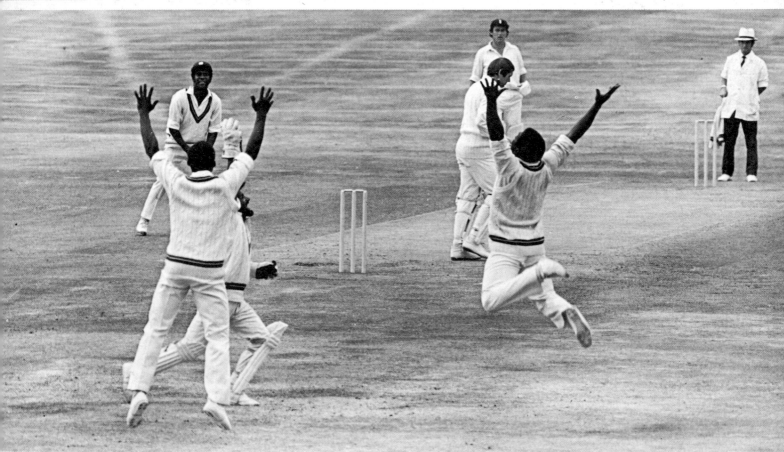

Greenidge scored his third century in a row and together with Fredericks (*top left*) put on 192 for the first wicket.

Greig (*right*) led England from the front with 116 and 76, Alan Knott also making a first innings 116.

Willis took the most prized wicket (*above*) when he bowled Richards in the second innings.

Balderstone falls to Roberts (*left*), caught by Murray, one of the five catches he took in England's second innings. West Indies won by 55 runs.

Dennis Amiss showed his liking for The Oval with 203. Purists disliked the 'shuffle' he developed to counteract the West Indian pace bowlers.

Fredericks (*above*) and Greenidge (*right*) gave a display of power that can seldom have been experienced by any fielding side. They were unbeaten in the second innings, 182-0 declared.

West Indies had earlier made their highest total against England (687 for eight declared) — largely due to Viv Richards' second double century of the series. Richards was eventually dismissed for 291.

Woolmer is Holding's first victim, lbw.

Amiss took a little longer, bowled for 203.

Knott is bowled Holding for 50 (victim 7).

Much to the delight of the West Indies, Greig is bowled.

Knott loses his middle stump to Holding.

Selvey goes the very next ball, also bowled by Holding.

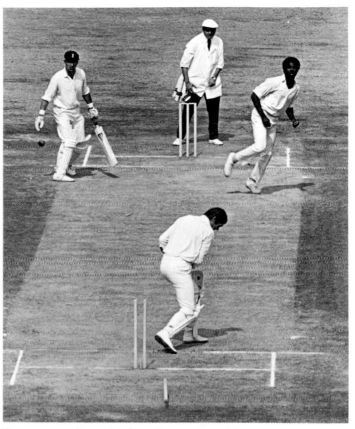

The stumps took a terrible battering, Balderstone bowled again.

On a wicket that, before the match, the experts had described as one to offer little to the bowlers, Holding's performance was little short of miraculous. He took 14 wickets in the match, nine of them bowled and two lbw; a reward for the virtue of bowling straight.

Solkar catches Brearley at short leg off Bedi (*above*).

Tony Greig quickly developed techniques to handle the Calcutta crowd. Here (*left*) he plays 'dead' immediately after an extremely explosive firework had been detonated just as Madan Lal came in to bowl. The crowd loved it.

An example of Kirmani's agility and the difficulty of playing Chandrasekhar (though fortunately for England, Chandra was not at his best during the series). Although Kirmani got a glove to the ball in the incident (*right*), he did not make the catch.

▶ Eden Gardens, Calcutta is one of the wonders of the cricketing world (*overleaf*). Every day sees a full house, but no one knows how many that is. Current estimates exceed 100,000.

John Lever (*left*) was involved in an unfortunate controversy when he was accused of applying Vaseline to the ball. Vaseline, however, is not a good polish but it did illustrate that caution in all matters is the best policy in India.

Mike Brearley (*right*) makes a brilliant catch at first slip to dismiss Viswanath off Underwood.

Tony Greig (*below*) followed his century at Calcutta with 54 and 41, and in winning this Test took an unbeatable lead in the series.

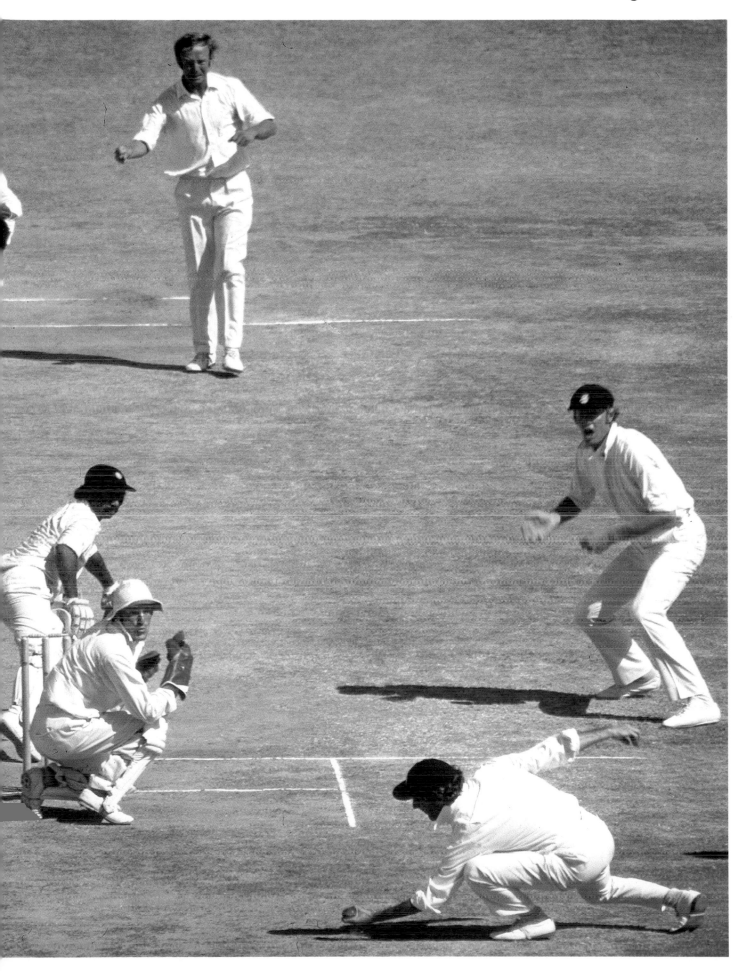

■1977

The Centenary Test at Melbourne was the perfect cricket match. Played in brilliant weather, with a cliff-hanging finish, watched by most of the surviving Australian and English Test players and superbly organized off the field, it provided a week that will never be forgotten by any who were fortunate enough to be present.

In the pre-Test line-up of current players and all the past captains (*right*), Rodney Marsh is talking to Sir Donald Bradman ; others are (*left to right*) ; Tony Greig, Ken Barrington, Bob Parish, Ray Steele, Greg Chappell and Jack Ryder.

O'Keeffe is caught by Brearley off Underwood (*below*).

Greig and Brearley dive left and right respectively (*facing page*) – Greig took the catch, Gilmour was the batsman and Old the bowler. Australia made 138 in their first innings.

Fletcher looks round in time to see Marsh catch him off Walker (*above*). England made only 95 and the organizers were wondering if the match would last three days.

Australia fought back in the second innings, Hookes (*below*) making a rapid 56 — it was his first Test — and McCosker, who had his jaw broken by Willis in the first innings, plays him during his 25 in the second (*left*).

The stands of the M.C.G. were well filled from the first day ; with space for 120,000 it is the largest cricket ground in the world.

Rodney Marsh, here driving Greig, became the first Australian wicket-keeper to score a century against England. Australia declared at 419.

Derek Randall made 174 and helped England to get within 45 runs of Australia's total. He hooks Lillee for 4 (*above left*) but opts not to accept the challenge (*above right*). Finally (*left*) he is caught by Cosier off O'Keeffe. The suspense at the end was tremendous, but Lillee took the last English wicket when he had Knott lbw (*right*). In one of those unlikely coincidences Australia's victory by 45 runs was by exactly the same margin as that of the match played 100 years previously.

1977/78

1st Test **England v. Australia** *Lord's*
2nd Test **England v. Australia** *Old Trafford*
3rd Test **England v. Australia** *Trent Bridge*
4th Test **England v. Australia** *Headingley*
5th Test **England v. Australia** *The Oval*

3rd Test **Pakistan v. England** *Karachi*

1st Test **West Indies v. Australia** *Port of Spain*
2nd Test **West Indies v. Australia** *Bridgetown*

By the time the 1977 series between England and Australia began, the shadow of Kerry Packer loomed large over establishment cricket. It was to remain there for several years until the rift in the game was healed and that dreadful word, Packerites, was allowed to disappear from cricket's vocabulary.

The first indication that something sinister was afoot came on May 9 during the Australians' rain-blighted match at Hove against Sussex, the county captained by Greig. By May 13, Greig had been deposed from the England captaincy – all that could be said in his favour was that he was an Englishman only by adoption – and it had been revealed that 18 Australian and 17 'overseas' players, the cream of the world's cricketers, would appear for Packer's World Series Cricket circus in Australia in 1977-78. Of those 18 Australians, 13 were in Greg Chappell's touring party. Greig, Knott, Snow and Underwood were the only England players involved, though others would join the breakaway group later. Boycott, it was learnt, had been approached but had declined the offer. His ambitions lay elsewhere.

Faced once more with a captaincy problem, England turned to Brearley, captain of county champions Middlesex and Greig's vice-captain in India. Whether or not to select the 'rebels' was solved by the decision that 'England sides this summer [should be chosen] strictly on merit'. With a full-strength Australian team already in the country, no one was going to suggest cutting off one's nose . . . And so it was that Greig, Knott and Underwood were called upon for the Jubilee Test at Lord's, the first in the latest contest for the Ashes.

With Pascoe generating real pace and Thomson and Walker obtaining life and movement, England were indebted to Woolmer and Randall for a first-innings total of 216. Chappell and Walters, the old hands, and Serjeant, on his début, looked to be building a commanding total for Australia on Saturday until Willis warmed English hearts on a grey day by dismissing all three, as well as Centenary Test century-maker Marsh. On Monday morning he ran through the tail to finish with seven wickets – the first time an England fast bowler had reaped such a reward in an innings since Snow did so in 1970-71 at Sydney, where Willis, at 21, played in his first Test. It had taken time for Willis to fulfil his promise, but at last England had a bowler to rank with the world's best for speed and hostility. They also had, in Brearley, a gifted leader, and if he rarely translated county form into Test runs, at Lord's he held firm in the second innings while Woolmer laid the foundations for his hundred and determined that the match would be drawn.

At Old Trafford, Woolmer was again in century form, becoming the first Englishman since Ken Barrington, in 1966, to score hundreds in successive innings against Australia – and also earning himself a Packer contract. There were substantial innings, too, from Randall and Greig, and England's 437 left Australia to score 140 to avoid an innings defeat. That they did so was due to the brilliance of Chappell, who struck a masterly hundred while partners came and went. No one seemed prepared, though many were capable, to play the necessary supporting role. The 82 runs required by England for victory were scored mostly by openers Amiss and Brearley, and England went ahead in the series.

Nor did it look as if the Australians would be able to overcome their opponents' advantage. Lacking match practice early in the tour because of rain, their batting had a brittleness about it that did not inspire confidence. As a team they were divided by the Packer issue, and it was noticeable that the composition of the Test team favoured WSC employees, irrespective of form. Thus Hughes, an exciting prospect, was played only in the last Test. In the field, concentration wavered at vital times, providing the unexpected sight of English fielders far outshining their Australian counterparts. Indeed, Brearley credited his victory at Old Trafford to the difference in the catching.

And it was a dropped catch in the third Test that probably decided the series. Boycott, recalled from his Yorkshire eyrie to replace Amiss, had taken three hours to gather 20 unsure runs when, having just run out Randall, favourite son of Trent Bridge, he was dropped at second slip off Pascoe. That would have made England 87 for six, with Pascoe firing on all cylinders; instead Boycott marched on to an inevitable century, Knott paced and passed him to three figures, and England took control. An unbeaten 80 in his second innings, to give England a 2-0 lead in the series, restored Boycott to full confidence, and in the fourth Test at Headingley he made Australia pay further with a steady 191, his 100th first-class hundred.

Newcomer Botham, who had announced his presence at Trent Bridge with five wickets in an innings, took another five at Headingley in Australia's first innings of 103. They batted with more conviction second time round but could not prevent England from recovering the Ashes on the fourth day with an innings victory. Rain, plus the fact that it could not affect the series, diminished the importance of the drawn Oval Test, in which the Australians gave one of their best performances. For many of them, as for some England players, it was their last appearance for their country before putting on Mr Packer's multi-colour night-clothes.

Now the problem of the Packer WSC players entered a new phase. For England and Australia there was no question of including these men in future Test sides, but not all other countries felt the need to be so dogmatic. When Australia met West Indies in March 1978, for example, the WSC season had finished and the crowd-drawing names were back home in the Caribbean, willing to play for West Indies. Opposing them was a second-, almost third-, string Australian side led by 42-year-old Bobby Simpson, who had last captained a Test side 10 years earlier; and after two Tests the inexperienced tourists had twice been bounced to defeat in three days. They were saved from being whitewashed by the decision of the West Indies Board to drop three WSC players from their third Test team in favour of players who would be available for a later tour of India. In the resulting brouhaha Clive Lloyd resigned as captain and 'out' with him went the other WSC West Indians. Packer himself flew in to play peacemaker, but the Board refused to accommodate the rebel players further and chose a new side.

The series now came alive as the Australians won the third Test through the fast bowling of Thomson and Clark and second-innings hundreds from Wood and Serjeant. Newcomer Williams and Gomes hit hundreds for West Indies, who went on to take the fourth Test, and the series, thanks to the fast-medium bowling of Holder and the spin (oh happy days) of Parry and Jumadeen. Australia were on the brink of victory in the fifth Test when crowd trouble stopped play late on the final day. When attempts to bowl the remaining overs of the mandatory last 20 on the next day were thwarted by the refusal of one umpire – and his stand-in – to co-operate, the match was abandoned.

Earlier in the season the new-look Australia, at home, had beaten India by three Tests to two in a fluctuating series which thrilled the Australian public and proved that Test cricket could still entertain without the star names. Furthermore, as Bedi and Chandrasekhar illustrated, the bowling did not have to be all biff-bang and bouncers to win matches. The Indian batsmen needed the first two Tests to get used to the speed and bounce of Thomson, though Gavaskar's class shone through. He hit hundreds in the first three Tests. India won the third and fourth Tests comprehensively, by 222 runs and by an innings, and looked like pulling off an amazing victory in the fifth by amassing 493 in their second innings. They fell short by only 47 runs in a match that Australia had set off with a first innings of 505, Simpson hitting his second hundred of the series and Yallop his first in Test cricket.

England, touring Pakistan, could not produce such exciting fare; nor could their opponents. Tedium was the staple diet on grassless, slow-turning wickets and all three Tests were drawn. Unruly crowd behaviour marred the first Test;

Kerry Packer, whose television and publishing empire provided the necessary financial backing for World Series Cricket.

cynics might suggest that the long-awaited hundred (9 hours 17 minutes) of Mudassar Nazar did. Boycott did not help either, spreading his 50 over 4 hours 50 minutes. In the second Test he scored 100 not out, though Brearley had to claim the optional last half-hour for him to do so after Boycott had begun his innings the previous evening. It was a different story at Karachi: so placid was the pitch and a result so impossible that Boycott and Wasim Raja agreed to end the match an hour early. It was significant that there were no demonstrations at this decision.

Boycott was captaining England because Brearley had broken his arm in a one-day game several days earlier. However, it was the more diplomatic Brearley who dealt with the issues which preceded this final Test. Throughout the tour, many Pakistanis had expressed dissatisfaction that their WSC players – Majid, Zaheer, Imran and Mushtaq – were not brought home for the Tests. (When it was rumoured that Packer would make them available, the selectors named 23 players for the first Test and announced their eleven only at the last minute.) At Karachi, the matter finally came to a head with the appearance at net practice of Zaheer, Imran and Mushtaq. Brearley, on behalf of the England players, expressed opposition to the selection of WSC players and it was thought they might even refuse to play if the 'Packerstanis' were chosen. In the event they were not, and the two teams settled down to the dull business of not losing.

England then went on to New Zealand, where Boycott, having fulfilled his ambition to captain his country, suffered the ignominy of leading England to their first-ever defeat by New Zealand. At Wellington, fast bowlers Richard Hadlee (six for 26) and Collinge bowled out England for a paltry 64 to secure an historic victory by 72 runs. At Christchurch, Botham's powerfully hit hundred, eight wickets and three catches won England the second Test by 174 runs, and his rumbustious half-century enlivened a dreary draw at Auckland, where Howarth's hundred in each innings for New Zealand and Radley's eight-hour hundred for England negated the provision of a sixth day. Boycott, who had scratched the cornea of his right eye, watched the final two days of the series from behind dark glasses, little realising that they were to be his last as England's Test captain.

111

Greig lost the England captaincy because of his involvement with Kerry Packer, but along with the other players who had signed contracts, he was allowed to play in the series. Here Pascoe unsettles Greig with a lifting delivery (*left*) and then bowls him three balls later (*right*).

Brearley is caught by Robinson (*right*) just one run short of his half century, O'Keeffe the bowler.

Slips all-a-jumble, and a dispairing Greg Chappell as another catch goes down (*bottom right*).

Bob Woolmer was England's top scorer in both innings. He pulls O'Keeffe for 4 past an all too close Robinson at short leg (*below*).

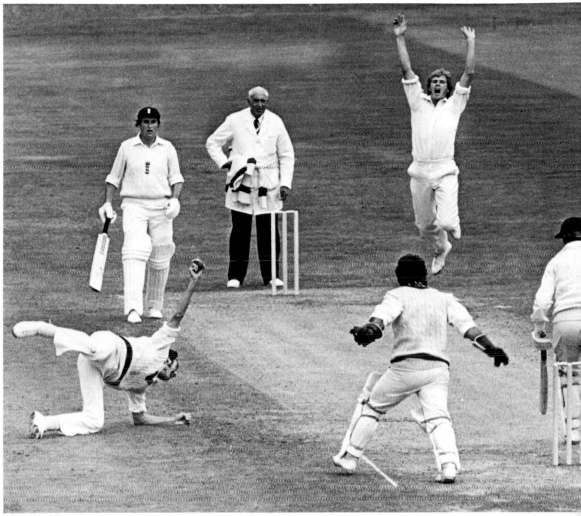

Mike Brearley wearing his temple protector – the forerunner of current crash helmets and at the time subject of much comment. This Test was his second as England's captain and it was his first victory.

Ex-captain Greig, all set for a century, is caught and bowled by Walker (*right*).

Underwood watches as the ball, bowled by Max Walker, just hits the stumps without dislodging a bail (*left*).

Greg Chappell (*above*), now captaining an Australian side split into two camps (Packer and non-Packer), does his best to hold them together with a determined century. But to no avail ; England won by nine wickets.

Derek Randall, England's latest batting success, played in a Test match for the first time in front of his home crowd at Trent Bridge, where he is more than usually adored. Geoff Boycott came in from the cold and played for England for the first time since 1974. Sad it was then, when there was a muddle over a single, and Randall was run out for 13. Boycott confirmed his return with a century, although he was dropped in the slips when he had made only 20, and England were 87 for 5. He went on to bat on each day of the five day Test.

Ian Botham announced his entry into Test cricket with five wickets in his first innings. His haul included Chappell, Walters and Marsh (*above*).

Alan Knott was England's top scorer with 135 and he became the first wicket keeper to score 4,000 Test runs.

Knott catches Marsh down the leg side off Botham (*above*), a superb example of Knott's agility and timing.

Boycott, too, exercised a unique sense of timing when he made his 100th first class century in a Test match against Australia in front of his own Headingley crowd. This is the on drive that produced the hundredth run (*facing page*).

Randall (*right*), makes no mistake in catching Marsh to give England the Test match and the Ashes. This is more than can be said of the photographer, who having taken this photograph, managed to miss the cart-wheel that immediately followed.

5th Test
England v. Australia
The Oval

▶ Storm clouds pass over north London, happily avoiding The Oval. The first day was lost to rain, and the Test match is about to start late on the second morning. Part of the Houses of Parliament can be glimpsed to the left of the gasometer, and Boycott is taking guard. Altogether, more than 11 hours were lost to rain in a match that inevitably ended as a draw.

■1977/78

Brearley's arm had been broken earlier in the week, and he had flown home leaving Boycott to realize a long-cherished ambition — to captain England. Like the two previous Tests in the series, this one was a draw. No fewer than six English batsmen were lbw in their first innings, one of them was Taylor (*below*) lbw Abdul Qadir. Things livened up a bit when Willis bowled to Shafiq Ahmed (*right*) and Mudassar Nazar (*below right*) made 76 to follow his slowest century in all first class cricket at Lahore.

The match was watched by three Pakistani players on leave from Packer's Circus, sent over from Australia in the hope of selection.

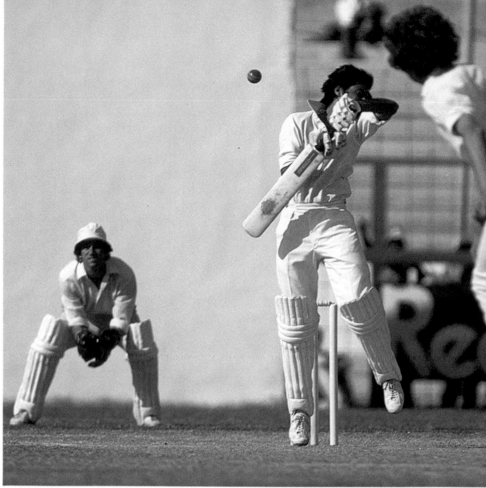

The restive crowd kept themselves amused with a dust bag fight.

Wasim Bari shows what he felt about the Test.

■1978

Following Kerry Packer's first season the West Indies were free to pick from all their players, while Australia sent an inexperienced side, captained by the long retired Bobby Simpson. The Australians were dismissed for a mere 90 in their first innings, Simpson (*below*) being out for 0 and Toohey (*right*) being struck a terrible blow off the top edge while attempting to hook Roberts. The West Indies pace attack (*below right*) had a field day ; left to right, Croft (four for 15), Garner (three for 35) and Roberts (two for 26).
The wicket had improved by the second innings (*far right*) and Serjeant (*top*) and Wood (*bottom*) — both hooking Roberts — looked more confident. Nevertheless Australia lost by an innings in three days.

Graham Yallop tries out a crash helmet against Joel Garner. This was the first Test match in which a full helmet was worn by batsmen.

Yardley, who made a brave 74, did not bother with a helmet and probably wished that he had — he goes down after being hit by Garner.

The West Indies managed to infuriate Jeff Thomson by bowling short to Jim Higgs, who is in the Chandrasekhar class of number 11 batsmen. Thommo bowled what many consider his fastest ever spell at the West Indian batsmen that first evening. Greenidge (*left*) suffered bouncers (*top*), then an over-exuberant appeal – which all but Simpson and the umpire insisted was out (*middle*) – and finally succumbed, caught by Cosier (*bottom*). Richards was another victim, who was eventually caught hooking, but not before being dropped, and playing an amazing lofted drive off the back foot which nearly went for six (*above*).

127

Yardley's stump appears to be taking a walk as Garner uproots it in the Australian second innings.

The West Indies target was a mere formality, Greenidge (80 not out) hitting the ball to all parts inside and outside the ground.

1978/79

1st Test **England v. Pakistan** *Edgbaston*
2nd Test **England v. Pakistan** *Lord's*
3rd Test **England v. Pakistan** *Headingley*

1st Test **England v. New Zealand** *The Oval*
2nd Test **England v. New Zealand** *Trent Bridge*
3rd Test **England v. New Zealand** *Lord's*

2nd Test **Pakistan v. India** *Lahore*

2nd Test **Australia v. England** *Perth*
3rd Test **Australia v. England** *Melbourne*
4th Test **Australia v. England** *Sydney*

While negotiations continued in an attempt to bring peace and unity to cricket, England played host to their opponents of the past winter, Pakistan and New Zealand. The former, acutely aware of England's stance, did not include their World Series Cricket players and so lacked the strength and experience to compete on equal terms with England in England. New Zealand, who had the better half of the summer, were able to call on all their players with the exception of the prolific Turner, who chose instead to remain with his county, Worcestershire. England, looking ahead to a series in Australia, took the opportunity to develop a team to defend the Ashes. Brearley returned as captain for both series after Boycott had broken his thumb while leading England in a one-day game against Pakistan.

Except in the drawn third Test at Headingley, where rain and bad light reduced play to ten and a half hours and Sadiq went out to bat eight times in an innings of 97, compiled over four days, Pakistan were overwhelmed. At Edgbaston, where Old dismissed four batsmen in five balls, they lost by an innings and 57 runs; at Lord's, where Botham hit his second hundred of the series and took eight for 34 in Pakistan's second innings, the margin was an innings and 120 runs. Each defeat came in four days, in effect two and a half at Lord's;

disheartening results for an inexperienced team robbed of match practice throughout their tour by wretched weather. In addition, Sarfraz broke down after only six overs of the first Test and did not play until the third, where he emphasised his importance to the side with five wickets in England's 119 for seven.

The weather apart, the series was soured by the incident in the first Test in which Willis, going round the wicket, injured Iqbal Qasim, usually a tail-ender but now proving to be a stubborn night-watchman. Willis, who had earlier been warned for bowling too many bouncers, as well as for running on the pitch, had given Iqbal a torrid time in his opening overs, and this time he got through his defence, striking him a sickening blow to the face. As a consequence, it was agreed that the captains should exchange lists of non-recognised batsmen at whom bouncers would not be bowled, although Brearley defended Willis's tactics, stating that 'a night-watchman expects to be treated like a batsman'.

The International Cricket Conference, seven weeks later, attempted to impose a limit of one bouncer an over, under an experimental law. However, in Pakistan later that year, Gavaskar was subjected to such a barrage of short-pitched deliveries from Sarfraz and Imran that

he called his captain, Bedi, on to the field to protest.

The New Zealanders, whose expectations were high after their success at home, were disappointing and lost all three Tests. They were handicapped by injuries to their seam bowlers, but dropped catches wasted hard-earned advantages. Gower, an exciting left-hander introduced to Test cricket against Pakistan, was let off twice in mid-innings at The Oval and went on to his maiden hundred. Similarly, Boycott, who for the second year in succession returned to the England side with a hundred at Trent Bridge, was dropped at the start of that innings. Brearley, who was experiencing a disastrous run with the bat, put himself down the order at Trent Bridge and quietened his critics, temporarily, with a half-century. At Lord's, it was New Zealand's batsmen who let them down, shot out for 67 by the speed of Willis and the swing of Botham, who in the twin series claimed 37 wickets.

With his remarkable hitting, his devastating spells with the ball and his inspirational prehensile fielding, Botham at 23 had established himself as a world-class match-winner. Just how vital he was to England's performance was noticeable during his absence, injured, from the opening matches in Australia later in 1978. Only when he came back into the side did England win their first match, having already gone down to South Australia; literally so in the case of Radley, who was hit over the eye by a fast bowler called Hogg and fell on to his stumps. When Hogg was chosen for the first Test, England's batsmen knew they would not emerge unscathed from the battle for the Ashes, even though Thomson, forbidden by a court order to join WSC until April, had chosen to sit out the summer.

Rarely, if ever, has such importance been attached to an Ashes series. The Test matches were in direct competition to the Packer series and, as their domestic Sheffield Shield matches were sparsely attended, the Australian authorities were desperate for large crowds to boost their flagging finances. Since the advent of Packer, Test players' fees had increased appreciably, and in England Test matches had been sponsored for the first time, by Cornhill Insurance. The Australians, too, had sponsors, but if they were to keep them they needed evidence that the authorised version of the game held greater appeal than Packer's. Sadly, as the series swung England's way, a fickle public looked elsewhere for their entertainment. The trumpeter who played the Last Post as England wrapped up the sixth Test on the fourth day was sounding for more than Australia's overwhelming defeat in the series by five Tests to one. He was foreshadowing the demise of Australian cricket unless the establishment could come to terms with Packer and Australia could once more field a winning team.

Yet in Hogg Australia had a genuinely quick bowler who, in normal circumstances, would have had the Aussies braying for blood. He had seven wickets at Brisbane, 10 at Perth, 10 at Melbourne, where Australia won for the only time, six in Sydney, where Randall stood between Australia and victory, seven at Adelaide, and finally one at Sydney for a record 41 wickets in Anglo-Australian Tests. What Australia did lack was a solid batting line-up, overall application, and a captain who could apply pressure as England's did. Yallop, who hit centuries in the first and last Tests, did his best as Australia's captain but had neither the experience nor the resources.

England's strength, in addition to Brearley's leadership, was their team spirit, with every member of the side making a contribution to its success.

The fielding, as one had come to expect since Greig inspired such an improvement in India, was outstanding. Botham, Brearley and Hendrick excelled close to the bat, Gower and Randall closed down the cover and mid-wicket areas, and Taylor's wicket-keeping drew comparison with England's finest. Taylor's gritty 97 at Adelaide first saved and eventually won the fifth Test for England. Miller, his Derbyshire colleague, came on enormously both as a batsman and as an off-spinner, finishing the series equal with Botham as England's leading wicket-taker. The successful use of their two off-spinners – Emburey was the other – was a feature of England's attack.

Only the batting gave cause for continued concern. Gower delighted all who saw his sweetly timed stroke-play – 'a minor genius', said Brearley – and Randall relished once more the fast Australian wickets. But there was only one opening partnership of 50 or more. Boycott, who had recently been relieved of the Yorkshire captaincy, had an unhappy tour personally; Gooch looked happier lower down the order, and Brearley's batting form remained elusive. However, in the fourth Test at Sydney it was Brearley who stayed with Randall as Australia's first-innings lead of 142 was eroded, and England, by giving Emburey and Miller enough runs to play with, were able to turn the tables and win by 93 runs.

So it was that England retained the Ashes. But their victories were to have another result as well: capitulation by the Australian Board. At the end of April 1979, they announced that they had 'granted PBL Sports the exclusive right, for a term of 10 years, to promote the programme of cricket organised by the Board and to arrange the televising and merchandising in respect of that programme'. As the contract for that televising would go to Channel 9, cricket's revolution was over. Packer had got what he wanted.

That the Packer problem was intrinsically an internal Australian one, which had been allowed to escalate on an international scale, had become even more obvious when, in October 1978, Pakistan chose their WSC players for the three-Test series against India, the first time the countries had met since January 1961. Zaheer Abbas, one of the Packer men, hit 583 runs in five innings to average 194.33 as Pakistan won 2-0, and such was the strength of the home team's batting that they were never

once bowled out. Javed also averaged over 100. Of the Indians, only Gavaskar matched the Pakistan batsmen; his compatriots too often failed to apply the technique or temperament necessary to cope with the short-pitched bowling directed at them.

The Packer players were also available when Pakistan toured New Zealand and Australia from January to March. Two of the three Tests in New Zealand were drawn, Pakistan winning the first by 128 runs, and again New Zealand's catching let them down. In Australia, the two Tests were shared, Pakistan taking the first thanks to a remarkable performance by Sarfraz, who took seven wickets for one run from 33 deliveries after Australia, with seven wickets in hand, had wanted just 77 runs for victory. In the second Test, Sarfraz was involved in the controversial dismissal of non-striker Hilditch, who was given out, handled the ball, after helpfully picking up a return to the bowler. Earlier in the same match Sikander Bakht, again the non-striker, had been run out by the bowler when backing up too soon. As prize-money was increasing, so too was sportsmanship diminishing.

West Indies had to tour India when their WSC players were playing for Packer in Australia. They met Gavaskar in outstanding form, so too was Viswanath, his brother-in-law, and they found that India had two seam bowlers in Ghavri and Kapil Dev who did more than take the shine off the ball for the spinners. Kapil Dev, with an unbeaten 126 in the fifth Test, plus two half-centuries elsewhere, was making strong claims to be India's Botham. He won them the fourth Test – the only one of the series not drawn – by taking seven wickets in the match and, when India were 84 for six and needed another 41 to win, hitting 26 of them.

Gavaskar's 732 runs in the series included a double-hundred in the first Test, a hundred in each innings in the third, and a fourth century in the fifth Test. Viswanath and Vengsarkar each took two Test hundreds off the pace-orientated West Indian attack and Mohinder Amarnath and Gaekwad one each. Kallicharran, the captain, Bacchus and Williams reached three figures for a West Indian side whose true strength can be gauged properly from the fact that Kallicharran was its only member to play for West Indies against Australia in the PBL-programmed season a year later.

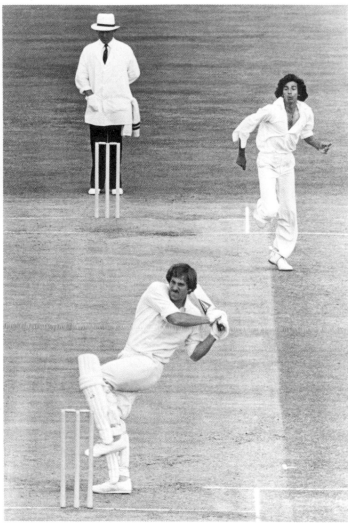

David Gower (*top left*) hits his first ball in Test cricket for 4.

Ian Botham (*top*), here hooking Sikander Bakht, made a century.

Chris Old took seven wickets in Pakistan's first innings and Sadiq gave the crash helmet its first outing on an England Test ground (*left*).

Nightwatchman Iqbal Qasim is hit in the face by a bouncer from Bob Willis. An unhappy and controversial moment (*right*).

England won the match by an innings.

Use of the crash helmet, still looking like the motor cycle type, spread to the England side. Brearley (*left*) earned a certain degree of ridicule at the time as the Pakistan bowlers were not considered quick enough to warrant such precautions. Miller (*above*) is well caught by Miandad and Botham (*below*) made another hundred; Miandad has no intention of of attempting to catch this one.

Not content with his century, Botham scythed his way through the Pakistan second innings. Here, Roope catches Talat Ali for 40.

Wasim Raja is caught and bowled by Botham, one of seven victims for 14 runs on the last day.

Botham made the ball swing prodigiously and it is hard to see how anyone could have played him. Wasim Bari is caught by Taylor.

The last Test of the series was virtually a wash-out. The umpires Bird and Palmer making fruitless inspections of the wicket most of the time (*right*).

During the time that play was possible, Sadiq Mohammad batted well for 97 (*lower right*).

Mohsin Khan was the second highest scorer before he was lbw to Willis for 41 (*below*).

Hadlee found The Oval wicket unhelpful — as have most other fast bowlers. Frustration as much as anything else was behind this appeal.

Mark Burgess, the New Zealand captain, kept Howarth company, here he manages to evade the grasp of Edmonds.

David Gower completed his maiden Test century (*facing page*).

Edgar is bowled by Edmonds (*left*) in the second innings. Edmonds took four for 20 in 34 overs, which left England the comparatively simple target of 138.

Boycott once again reappeared at Trent Bridge, and once again he was dropped early on (this year when he had made 2). Here he has mishooked Bracewell and Edwards has just failed to catch him. Boycott went on to make 131 helping England to a commanding lead. New Zealand lost by an innings.

Howarth (*left*) was easily New Zealand's most successful batsman in the series. He made 123 and New Zealand took a first innings lead.

Botham and Willis settled things in New Zealand's second innings – Burgess is caught Hendrick bowled Botham (*right*).

Hadlee is run out, as Botham, sprinting down the wicket, manages to hit the stumps (*below*).

■1978

India and Pakistan resumed playing Test cricket for the first time in 17 years. Visas, usually very difficult to obtain, were to be had for the asking and the presentation of a valid Test match ticket. This enabled the Sikhs (*right*) to cross the border into Pakistan for the day to watch the cricket.

They may have wondered if it was worth it when India were dismissed on an unusually green Lahore wicket for 199. Zaheer alone made a majestic 235 for Pakistan (*below*), contributing to a total of 539 for six declared.

Javed Miandad did not do so well, here being bowled by M. Amarnath for 35, but the Pakistan lead was eventually decisive.

India recovered dramatically in the second innings. Gavaskar, seen here making Miandad uncomfortable, was unlucky to be out for 97.

Bedi is bowled by Sarfraz in the second innings and Pakistan scent victory (*right*).

The setting at Gaddafi stadium in Lahore is a beautiful one (*facing page*). Gavaskar is facing Sarfraz in the second innings.

By Islamic convention, ladies are seldom seen unescorted in public – at the cricket ground they have their own stand. The barbed wire is all round the ground to discourage pitch invasions (*below*).

England toured Australia in competition with Kerry Packer's World Series. Gower made a century in spite of this narrow squeak (*left*), Maclean is the wicket keeper. Umpire Tom Brooks (*above*) has just given Wood out — a controversial decision which partly led to the announcement of his retirement. Boycott, who was having a miserable time off the field, having just been replaced as Yorkshire's captain, drops Wood (*below*) as he mis-hooked Botham. The ball came to him high and straight out of the glaring Perth sun. Cruelly for Boycott, exactly the same thing happened a few balls later.

Australia beat England, but were still 2-1 down in the series. Boycott found the bowling about as unfriendly as the crowds. Here he sways inside a bouncer from Hogg. Hogg finished the series with 41 wickets, easily the most successful bowler on either side.

Derek Randall (*facing page*) was largely responsible for giving the England spinners a chance to win this match. He fought his way to 150, often in extreme heat – the temperature was over 100°F for most of his innings.

The dressing room scene as Randall (*centre*) takes a well deserved rest. Brearley (*left*) and Miller (*right*) also watch the closing stages of the England innings on television, which gives a better view than that from the window.

Higgs is lbw to Emburey (*below*) and the Australian collapse is almost complete – Emburey and Miller taking seven wickets between them.

1979/80

1st Test **England v. India** *Edgbaston*
2nd Test **England v. India** *Lord's*
3rd Test **England v. India** *Headingley*
4th Test **England v. India** *The Oval*

2nd Test **Australia v. England** *Sydney*
3rd Test **Australia v. West Indies** *Adelaide*
3rd Test **Australia v. England** *Melbourne*

Jubilee Test **India v. England** *Bombay*

The confusion was over, it was time for the profusion. Integral to the terms of settlement between the Australian Board and World Series Cricket was a triangular limited-overs tournament between Australia and two overseas sides, plus a twin three-Test series. For 1979-80 the decree went out that West Indies, the world one-day champions, and England, holders of the Ashes, should visit Australia, regardless of the fact that India had earlier been invited to share a tour of Australia with England. To add injury to this insult, India were then asked to accommodate a visit by Australia as early as September so that the Australians would be home in time for the PBL programme.

On reflection, it seems as if the Indians did nothing but play Test matches. Of the 29 Tests played between July 1979 and March 1980, 17 involved India. It was not surprising that their tour to the West Indies had to be cancelled because players were unavailable. And yet they could hardly have begun this arduous programme in less auspicious circumstances, having failed to win a match in the World Cup which preceded their four-match series in England. Even Sri Lanka, yet to be elevated to Test-playing status, had beaten them.

England, however, entered the first Test full of confidence. Although they had lost to a full-strength West Indies in the World Cup final, they had not been disgraced. Brearley and Boycott had put on a century opening partnership against Roberts, Holding, Croft and Garner. Kapil Dev and Ghavri would present fewer problems, and the wily Chandrasekhar could not do himself justice because of an ankle injury. Boycott began the England innings at his own pace, but Gooch, still at Number 4, got it moving with an aggressive 83. When he was out, Gower joined Boycott in a stand of 191 before Boycott succumbed to the apparently tireless Kapil Dev for 155. Miller then kept Gower company as the young left-hander compiled an effortless, unbeaten double-century, whereupon Brearley declared at 633 for five.

Gavaskar and Viswanath batted almost through the first two sessions on Saturday, but Randall's brilliance at mid-wicket ran out Gavaskar, there was a collapse, and by the close India had followed on 336 in arrears. With the score 227 for four on the fourth day it looked as if England might have to bat a second time. Then Botham struck – four for 10 in five overs – and immediately England had won by an innings and 83 runs with a day to spare.

Botham was again to the fore at Lord's, taking five wickets in a Test innings for the 10th time as India were rushed out on the first day for 96; and on the Monday he claimed his 100th Test wicket after just two years and nine days of Test cricket – then the shortest time on record. England, for whom Gower was brilliant until he lost his concentration and his off-stump after hitting 82 off 95 balls, amassed 419 for nine, and by luncheon on the fourth day India were batting to avoid another innings defeat. Chauhan and Gavaskar began the holding operation, then Viswanath and Vengsarkar settled in for a long stay, securing the draw with defiant hundreds and occasional help from the rain.

At Lord's, most of Friday's play had been washed out by spectacular summer storms; at Headingley Botham and Randall had to wait from early Thursday afternoon until Monday morning to resume their innings. Botham spent the weekend on nine. He went to lunch on Monday with 108 runs by his name, just failing to hit 100 runs before lunch but having entertained the faithful with some of the most devastating hitting seen in England. A sweep off Bedi was retrieved from the car park; a pulled six off Kapil Dev brought up his hundred. He dominated the morning with a presence that suggested both Olivier and Marciano, stroking one four with classical timing, despatching another with savagery. In all, in an innings of 137, he hit five sixes and 16 fours, and had he not been bravely caught by Ghavri, going for his 22nd boundary, he would have reached his 1,000th run in Test cricket. He had to wait until The Oval for that.

Headingley having been drawn, India could square the series by winning at The Oval, and they came so close to an impossible victory that virtually everyone was willing them to achieve it. Set to score 438 in 500 minutes after Boycott's seven-hour hundred had allowed Brearley ample time to ponder over his declaration, India began the final day at 76 without loss. The diminutive Gavaskar's stature grew in proportion to an innings resplendent with immaculate strokes, but Chauhan's adhesive style was less appropriate to the run-chase. It needed the arrival of Vengsarkar to stimulate the innings, and at tea India were 304 for one, wanting another 134. However, Brearley slowed the over-rate and India still required 110 when the final 20 overs began.

At 365 for one, Botham dropped Vengsarkar and it seemed that the Kindly Ones were smiling on the Indians. Instead they were laughing up the sleeves of their gowns. In the last 12 overs, Botham caught Vengsarkar, ran out Venkataraghavan, and took three wickets including that of Gavaskar for a peerless 221. By the final over the target was down to 15 runs. With three balls to go all four results were possible: win to either side, tie or draw. Ultimately it was the draw, India finishing nine runs short with two wickets in hand. Seven days later they were taking the field at Madras for the first Test against Kim Hughes' Australians.

As they had for the World Cup, Australia toured without their WSC players. No one had experience of Indian conditions, and Hughes, Border and Yallop were the only batsmen who looked capable of playing the long innings so necessary there. Five Indians hit hundreds in the six-Test series, with Gavaskar, now captaining his country, and Viswanath getting two each. Kapil Dev was India's leading bowler, twice capturing five wickets in an innings and finishing with 28 wickets. Dymock, Australia's leading bowler, took 24 wickets, but half of these came in the third Test, which India won by 153 runs. They emphasised their superiority by winning the sixth Test by an innings and 100 runs with a day to spare. The other four Tests were drawn.

While the Australians returned home, many of them to the anonymity of domestic cricket, the Indians had but a fortnight's break before embarking on another six-Test series, this time against a much-troubled Pakistan. And once more they emerged victorious by two Tests to nil. In contrast to their opponents, team spirit was high among a side which had played together for more than six months. Gavaskar again averaged over 50, and Kapil Dev, with 32 wickets in the series, increased his tally of Test wickets to 100. His time for reaching three figures – one year and 107 days – comfortably beat Botham's record, and in the same game, the sixth Test, he also became the fastest to achieve the Test match 'double' when he hit his 1,000th run.

If Kapil Dev, having just turned 21, had become a serious threat to Gibbs' world record of 309 wickets, there had re-emerged in Australia a bowler who was capable of extending that record. Dennis Lillee was again playing for his country, as were Greg Chappell, Thomson, Marsh and other World Series cricketers. Indeed, with the exception of Kallicharran, Hughes, Border and Hogg, the drawn first Test at Adelaide between Australia and West Indies might have been a WSC match. Even the bouncers were much in evidence, which made the hundreds of Hughes and Chappell all the more meritorious. Yet even they were overshadowed by Richards, whose 140 was the first of several powerful innings he composed in the short series.

Australia's bowlers must have been thankful that the itinerary alternated their opponents, so allowing them a crack at England's more temperate batsmen in between the indulgences of the West Indians. Lillee, Australia's leading bowler in both series, had 12 wickets at 30.41 against West Indies but 23 at 16.86 against England. Now 30, he had cut his pace but not his effectiveness or his hostility. His action was still beautiful to watch, and he had added a deadly leg-cutter to his formidable arsenal.

Australia's batsmen, reinforced by Ian Chappell for three Tests, also greatly appreciated a respite from the unending West Indian pace quartet that took 55 of the 56 Australian wickets that fell. In contrast, Australia lost but 46 wickets to England, with Botham (19) and Underwood (13 at 31) the only double-figure wicket-takers. England's batsmen, as well as their bowlers, had a sorry series, Botham hitting the only hundred although Gooch, Gower and Boycott went close. Much interest was taken in Boycott's first innings against Lillee since 1972, and their initial confrontation, at Perth, saw honours even. Boycott was lbw to him for 0 in the first innings and carried his bat through the second for 99.

Perhaps the real difference between the touring teams lay in their approach to the limited-overs-plus-Test-matches tour. England viewed it rather as a visit to the English seaside and took something (or someone) for all seasons. The tour, to them, was in two distinct phases. The West Indians simply got on with their game, with the result that they outplayed England in the final of the limited-overs tournament and overwhelmed Australia by 10 wickets and by 408 runs in the two decided Tests. England, on the other hand, were beaten by Australia by 138 runs, by six wickets in four days after being inserted on a rain-affected pitch, and by eight wickets. The Ashes, however, were not at stake, much to the frequently and vociferously expressed displeasure of the home crowd. England, unlike West Indies, also refused to play their Tests without any rest day, as whimmed by the TV moguls.

The three countries then went separate ways, England stopping over at Bombay to celebrate the golden jubilee of the Indian Board. It allowed Botham the opportunity to renew his assault on India's bowlers with another hundred and on their batsmen with 13 wickets for the match as England put the weary India to flight by 10 wickets with a day to spare.

West Indies, without Richards who had played in Australia with a painful back injury, found themselves up against a world-class fast bowler in Richard Hadlee and were shot out for 140 and 212 in the first Test in New Zealand. The home side, requiring 104 to win, lost nine wickets in the process but achieved a victory that was to decide the three-Test series in their favour. After their cricket in Australia, the West Indians were a lacklustre lot in New Zealand. Tempers were short, stumps were kicked out of the ground in anger, umpires were insulted, even assaulted, and at one stage it looked as if the West Indians were going home midway through the final Test. The strain was beginning to tell.

Later in the month Greg Chappell took his Australians to Pakistan, where they were spun to defeat by seven wickets at Karachi just a week after their arrival. At Faisalabad 999 runs were scored for the loss of only 12 wickets, Chappell and Taslim Arif enjoying double-hundreds; and at Lahore Border ensured another draw with a century in each innings. This third Test also produced Lillee's only three wickets of the series. His average – 101!

The series against India followed on the second Prudential World
Cup, and was restricted to four Tests. In the first innings, after the
slowest of starts, England galloped to 633 (for five declared), the
main run scorers being Boycott (155) and Gower (*above*) who was
a delight to watch for all of his 200 not out.
India started badly, and must have felt that they had no chance when
Gavaskar ran himself out (*right*), Randall being the fielder responsible.
Taylor is in the act of removing a stump—Willis shows his approval.

The instant of truth for the Indian wicket keeper, Reddy, as he is bowled by Hendrick. It appears that the ball is lodged between the stumps—but it is one of those freak photographs that are taken at the moment of impact, something that can be done only by mistake.

The match ended in a draw, thanks to the weather, which flooded much of the outfield to a depth of several inches. Vengsarkar and Viswanath ensured the Indian position when they both scored second innings centuries. For the photographers the greatest suspense was waiting for Botham to take the elusive 100th Test wicket. After much trying, he persuaded Gavaskar to edge this ball to Brearley at slip and thus becoming the quickest player to this landmark.

159

The weather won this match for the second year running. However Botham was now in pursuit of the quickest Test match 'double' and scored a century of quite monumental power, even by his own standards. The ball was hit to all parts of the Headingley area.

Having left himself three short of 1,000 Test runs, Botham wasted no time in cutting Bedi (*right*) to achieve this target — and the double— in only 21 Test matches.

As runs, wickets and time peter out for the Indians, Venkat is spectacularly run out — Bairstow helps the photograph.

4th Test
England v. India
The Oval

At one point it looked as if India were going to stage another mammoth fourth innings score to snatch victory from a seemingly hopeless situation. In the West Indies in 1976 they had scored 406 and won by six wickets, now they needed 438. They ended up only 9 runs short of their objective. The inspired force behind this was Gavaskar who hit a supreme 221, which was full of exciting strokes like this.

Tony Greig, (*left*) England's former captain and now working for Kerry Packer's TV station, returns to a familiar spot in his new role to give his daily comment on the pitch.

Greg Chappell (*right*) played a decisive second innings — his 98 not out ensuring an Australian victory by six wickets.

Underwood's 100th Australian victim in Tests was Ian Chappell (*below*), caught by Ian Botham.

West Indies confirmed their superiority in their last Test against Australia, winning by 408 runs. Clive Lloyd set the pace with a blistering 121 (*left*). Andy Roberts (*above*) attempts to run out Hughes – but as the bails had already come off he had to co-ordinate the collection of the ball and the removal of the stump. He failed. Australia fell to the combined attack of Roberts, Holding, Garner and Croft. Weiner (*below*) is caught by Murray off Roberts, the first to go in a second innings that produced only 165 runs.

Australia made a clean sweep of the parallel series against England. Gooch is run out just inches from his first ever Test century ; Hughes' throw (*facing page*) is on the point of hitting the stumps. Marsh and Botham have differing opinions (*top*) as Botham's second innings, 119 not out, gives something worth remembering. The term 'England collapse' (*above*) takes on a new, more literal, meaning.

Viswanath asks the umpire if he may withdraw the Indian appeal against Taylor, who had been given out, caught at the wicket (*left*).

It was a great match for Botham and Taylor. The latter took 10 catches in the match (a new Test record). He can be seen here (*below*) taking one of them, Gavaskar off Botham.

Botham took 13 wickets and made
114 – the best all round
performance ever in a Test match.

1980/81

1st Test **England v. West Indies** *Trent Bridge*
2nd Test **England v. West Indies** *Lord's*
3rd Test **England v. West Indies** *Old Trafford*
4th Test **England v. West Indies** *The Oval*
5th Test **England v. West Indies** *Headingley*

Centenary Test **England v. Australia** *Lord's*

1st Test **West Indies v. England** *Port of Spain*
2nd Test **West Indies v. England** *Georgetown*
3rd Test **West Indies v. England** *Bridgetown*

The month of April was not so cruel for England's weary cricketers in 1981. It brought relief; time to return home to the spring rain. Under a young and inexperienced captain they had gone south for the winter to the Caribbean islands to face the most demanding battery of fast bowlers in the history of Test cricket. For many of them it was a continuation of their summer series against the same opponents and so they were prepared, mentally if not always in terms of ability, for the struggle ahead. But no amount of planning could have prepared them for the long days of politicking that threatened the tour. Nor for the tragedy that robbed them of their assistant-manager and coach, Ken Barrington. Forced to retire from first-class cricket in 1968 because of a heart attack, he suffered another, fatal attack during the third Test at Bridgetown, Barbados.

There had been no second Test. The politicians of Guyana saw to that by deporting Robin Jackman, a replacement for the injured Willis, because he had played and coached in South Africa. This despite assurances given before the team left England that there would be no objection to players who had worked in South Africa. It was more than a decade since South Africa had played their last Test match, in 1969-70 against Australia, but the Republic's apartheid policies had once more become a threat to the unity of international cricket. A year later, West Indies would withdraw

their invitation to New Zealand's cricketers because that country had played host to South African *rugby* players.

It was not as if cricket hadn't enough problems without the eruption of one which had lain conveniently dormant. The preponderance of fast and fast-medium bowling was not only boring spectators; it was robbing them of cricket. In the fourth Test of the 1980 England-West Indies series, the combination of slow-walking, long-walking fast bowlers and the thoughtless meanderings of spectators behind the bowler produced only 129 overs from five sessions: an average of one over every four and three-quarter minutes. At Lahore, later in the year, West Indies managed just 73 overs on the first day of the first Test against Pakistan – and this without Holding!

The behaviour of players, too, was still causing concern. In the fourth Test of that Pakistan-West Indies series, Sylvester Clarke reacted to the crowd's pelting him with fruit by hurling a brick into an enclosure and knocking out a spectator. While from Australia came further evidence of the pressure players were enduring from the endless round of tours and Test matches. Sunil Gavaskar, given out lbw when he felt the ball had first made contact with the bat, took such exception to the decision that he instructed his partner, Chauhan, to leave the pitch with him, presumably intending to forfeit the match. Happily

for India, commonsense prevailed and they went on to win the match and square the series.

To India and New Zealand had fallen the twin tour of Australia, following which the Indians went on to New Zealand for another three-Test series. This they lost by virtue of a 62-runs defeat in four days at Wellington, giving New Zealand some compensation for their 2-0 defeat by Australia. Once again no rest days were scheduled in the Australian series, but Chappell's men provided their own by winning the first two Tests against New Zealand in three days. They also beat India in three days in the first Test of that series but kept the cameras rolling for all five days in the next two. Patil's courageous and aggressive 174 kept India alive at Adelaide, and at Melbourne Kapil Dev called upon his Botham-like qualities to win the match. Ignoring a strained thigh, he bowled unchanged for 17 overs on the final day to take five wickets as Australia, needing 143 to win, slumped from 24 for three to 83 all out. Doshi, despite a fractured foot, bowled 22 overs of steady left-arm spin, just as Yadav had toiled away in Australia's first innings with a similar injury. It was because of these injuries that Shastri, a tall, teenage left-arm spinner, was flown to New Zealand, where he claimed six for 63 on his Test début.

Although Chappell and Hughes hit double-hundreds against India, Wood took centuries off both tourists, and

Walters signalled his final season as a Test player with a hundred against New Zealand, the dominant character was Lillee. With 37 wickets from the twin series he had become Australia's leading wicket-taker with 251. At Lord's, at the end of the 1980 summer, he had accounted for the cream of England's batting with a display of his craft which graced the Test match held to celebrate 100 years of Test cricket in England. Pascoe, taking five for 15 in 32 deliveries, then wrapped up England's first innings. Boycott achieved self-satisfaction over Lillee in the second innings with a ground-out hundred which, while it drew the match, also stood as an indictment of England's disappointing attitude to what should have been a festival. The Australians, for whom Hughes was a delight with his range of strokes, tried to make it so in spite of the weather. England were incapable of doing so because Botham, who once could have transformed the game, appeared to have lost his magical powers.

Although he lacked any experience of the job, Botham had been appointed England's captain in May following Brearley's decision not to tour again. He had inherited a winning team on the wane, and both for himself and his players he needed a 'soft' series. What he received instead were consecutive series against West Indies, first at home and then in the Caribbean.

The series in England was decided by the first Test at Trent Bridge, won by West Indies with two wickets in hand. And yet, had vital catches been held, it could have gone England's way and Botham's captaincy would have begun in the ascendant. Haynes, who sustained the dramatic West Indian second innings, was dropped at slip when 23; Roberts, who saw West Indies home, was missed in the covers when 13 were needed and his countrymen's nerves were fraying. In each instance the unlucky bowler was Willis, who hauled England back into contention by producing speed, stamina and hostility that were thought beyond him. Such was his commitment that he was near tears as he left the ground.

Thereafter the weather determined drawn matches, and the West Indians had to be content with a superiority that England could match only by occasional personal performances. Gooch thumped an exhilarating hundred at Lord's and was England's leading run-getter in the series, followed by Boycott. Rose reaped dividends from his determination to attack the bowling. Willey was twice involved in rescue operations, the second time with Willis at The Oval, where England almost made West Indies follow on, took a first-innings lead of 105, and then collapsed from 20 for four to 92 for nine on the last day. This was Willis's last Test of the summer, for his fitness and form had fallen away since his heroic efforts at Trent Bridge. Gower was another casualty of lost form, omitted after the first Test but, like Willis, included in the touring party for the West Indies.

Had they not lost eight hours on the final two days at Lord's, 10 hours or more at Old Trafford, all of the third day at The Oval and the first and fourth days at Headingley, West Indies would have won more than one Test. But it can also be argued that they would have dismissed England quicker had they bowled more overs, or if they had included a genuine spin bowler. As it was, Lloyd relied on the relentless pace quartet to keep the game within the bounds of his batsmen, an essential policy because, after their 518 at Lord's, West Indies failed to pass 300 in the next three Tests. Richards, brutal in an assault which was breathtaking in its execution, and Haynes, more cautiously, hit hundreds in their first Test match at Lord's; but after that only Lloyd, on his county ground at Old Trafford, reached three figures. Lloyd was injured in the fourth Test and took no part in the fifth, thus providing an instance of one county, Somerset, supplying both Test captains, Botham and Richards, while the county captain, Rose, participated as a player. The umpires, too, had Somerset connections.

For Botham, the series brought no hundreds, no five wickets in an innings. His highest score was 57 in the first Test, his 13 wickets cost almost 30 runs each, though after Willis he was England's principal wicket-taker. Nor did matters improve for him in the West Indies. In the four Tests played he scored only 73 runs with a top score of 26; his 15 wickets, the most by an England bowler, cost 32.80 each. He was criticised for being overweight and unfit, and certainly his bowling lacked the natural, easy action associated with those days when success was plentiful. He looked to be holding himself back, almost as if his mind were elsewhere and the responsibilities he attached to the captaincy were inhibiting his instincts. This also showed in his fielding: catches once taken were now spilled.

But would another captain have been more successful? At home, having prepared for England's visit with a four-Test tour of Pakistan, where they won a series (1-0) for the first time, Lloyd's West Indians were nigh invincible. Croft had made enormous advances and, with his wide-of-the-crease delivery and late movement, he caused England's batsmen no end of problems. He took 24 wickets at 19 each and only in the final Test, when Gooch gloriously laid into him, was he mastered. Holding, as fluent in approach and as fast as he had ever been, gave Boycott the unsettling round-the-wicket treatment, and it is testimony to the Yorkshireman's technique and courage that, at 40, he was one of only four batsmen with a three-figure aggregate for the series. Gooch, Gower and Willey were the others. Richards, with two hundreds, and Lloyd were the major contributors in a powerful West Indies line-up which only in Bridgetown failed to score more than 400. Indeed, only there did they bat twice.

Decisively beaten by an innings at Port of Spain and by 298 runs at Bridgetown, England drew the fourth Test, thanks to rain and hundreds by Willey and Boycott, and the fifth, in which Gower (154 not out), Willey and wicket-keeper Downton resisted the West Indians throughout the final day. It was a day which gave rise to optimism for the future and helped erase, if gradually, the uncertainty and unhappiness which had hung over the tour. Nevertheless, as the team flew back to England over Easter, they were ready for the spring rain.

Ian Botham photographed in Guyana, just over half way through his ten Test series as captain of England against the West Indies.

The ground at Trent Bridge — at its best, a capacity crowd, glorious sunshine and a recently modernized pavilion.
Needing only 99 runs to win with eight wickets in hand at the start of the last day, the West Indies nearly didn't make it. Willis bowled England into a strong position and when Haynes was run out with 3 runs needed (*right*), the improbable seemed possible.

Andy Roberts on the follow through. He was the most successful of the West Indian bowlers (eight wickets) and hit the winning run.

Of the three centuries scored in the match Desmond Haynes' was the largest, setting a new West Indies record for Lord's, with 184. Richards is usually a difficult act to follow and on this occasion it was impossible. Nevertheless Haynes' contribution was vital.

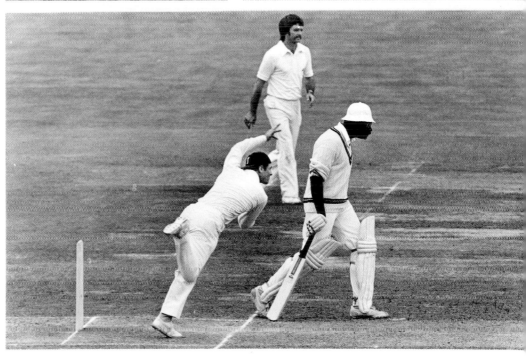

Graham Gooch (*upper left*) played his finest Test innings in very difficult circumstances, no other English batsman seemed to be able to cope with the West Indies attack.
Viv Richards (*upper right*) gave an exhibition of batting, which even by his exacting standards was little short of genius.
Boycott bowled seven overs for 11 runs (*right*).

It was apparent throughout the series that the Somerset pair, Botham and Richards, were engaged in their own private contest. Generally it would have to be said that Richards won fairly easily, but this round went to Botham.

Dilley bowled well for his three wickets. Here he celebrates the end of Bacchus.

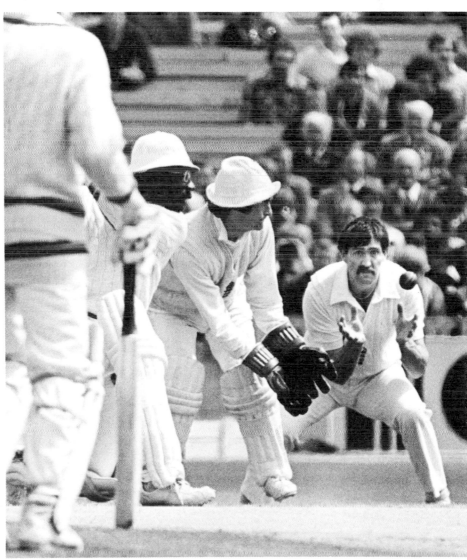

Lloyd had made 101 before he edged this ball from Emburey to Gooch at slip.

Peter Willey made a century (*right*) and with Willis put on 117 for the last second innings wicket. Before they came together, England were 92 for nine, and would surely have been beaten.

"Is everything OK in there?" Bacchus seems to be saying to the helmeted Boycott (*below*), in spite of the helmet, Boycott was hit badly enough to sustain a cut on the eyebrow from a Croft bouncer.

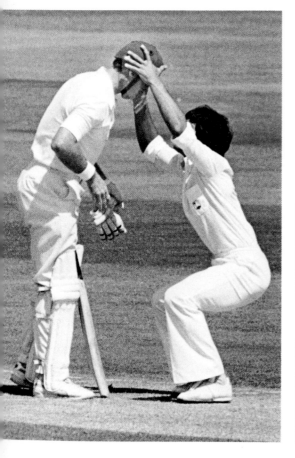

When it wasn't raining it was sunny enough to sit outside without a shirt – even if the seating is somewhat unconventional (*above*)

Richards, Greenidge, Kallicharran and an unidentifiable fourth slip with a not too enthusiastic appeal.

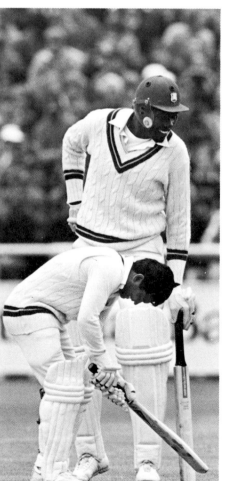

One of the lasting impressions of the summer – the West Indian over rate dropped to 12 overs an hour at times and with four bowlers taking run-ups like this, it was hardly surprising.

The long and the short of it (*left*); Joel Garner and Alvin Kallicharran.

Haynes is bowled by Emburey (*right*); he had struggled to 42 in very difficult conditions and won the Man of the Match award for his trouble.

Rose (*far right*) won nothing for his, as he fended off the hostile West Indian attack for an unbeaten 43.

The group of most of the England and Australian players, past and present, who were at Lord's for the Centenary Test.

The 164 players and officials patiently assembled on the morning of the second day of the Test. See page 221 for a key and caption.

Kim Hughes, who made 117 and 84 in a highly entertaining fashion, was Man of the Match. Here he has come down the wicket to Hendrick.

It was John Arlott's last Test match, and this was his last spell of broadcasting. The intrepid cameraman, intent on recording history, is some five stories above the ground-floor members.

Bairstow stumps Wood (*above left*) off Embury for 112.

Dennis Lillee (*left*) who together with Len Pascoe routed England in their first innings. Only Boycott, Gower, Gatting, Old and extras made double figures.

187

The glorious setting of the Queens Park Oval, Port of Spain — probably the most photogenic of all the current Test match grounds. West Indies amassed a first innings 426 with substantial contributions from all except Mattis who made 0, playing in his first Test.

England were overwhelmed by an innings and 79 runs.

■1981

1st Test
West Indies v. England
Port of Spain

West Indies once again used their line up of four top class fast bowlers, of whom Colin Croft (*right*) was the most successful. Before the match started there was considerable local feeling that Deryck Murray, a Trinidadian, had been unfairly dropped from the West Indian side. The match was poorly attended, but probably not as a result of this placard protest. Carnival was imminent, and in Trinidad even cricket takes second place to Carnival.

2nd Test
West Indies v. England
Georgetown

Bob Willis returned to England for a knee operation and Robin Jackman, the leading wicket taker in the 1980 English season was sent for. A day or so after his arrival, as a result of considerable political lobbying, the Guyanese Government announced that he was to be deported because of his South African connections. Jackman (*left*) with Graham Gooch is seen returning from the one-day international at Berbice. The England team moved out to Barbados the next day, where an anxious week was spent awaiting a decision from the remaining countries in the West Indies as to whether or not the tour would continue. The team manager A.C. Smith holds the microphone for an ITN interview with Jackman (*below*) — instant censorship at the flick of a switch?

A rare enough event, and good reason for celebration ; Dilley has dismissed Richards for 0 (*above*). Jackman took three wickets and West Indies were all out for 265. Any euphoria was short lived as Boycott faced Holding's first over, bowled at tremendous pace. Boycott looks back (*right*) to see his stump cart-wheeling away. Gooch followed later (*below*), bowled by Garner for 26 and England were all out for a first innings 122.

Following the saddest cricket news that Ken Barrington, the much loved and admired assistant manager, had died in his hotel during the night — the England team struggled on. Richards (*far left*) and Lloyd (*left*) took West Indies to an unassailable lead. Barbados personality King Dial, who kept the English tour visitors guessing as to what he would wear next (*above*) attempts to lend some cheerfulness to the proceedings.

1981/82

1st Test **England v. Australia** *Trent Bridge*
2nd Test **England v. Australia** *Lord's*
3rd Test **England v. Australia** *Headingley*
4th Test **England v. Australia** *Edgbaston*
5th Test **England v. Australia** *Old Trafford*
6th Test **England v. Australia** *The Oval*

1st Test **India v. England** *Bombay*

3rd Test **Australia v. Pakistan** *Melbourne*

If the decade from 1972 to 1982 developed as that of the fast bowler, it was in particular the decade of Dennis Lillee. When he arrived in England in May 1981, he ranked sixth among the world's leading wicket-takers. Some 10 months later he limped out of the third Test in New Zealand with a cartilage injury, having in the interim passed Gibbs' world record and extended his own to 328 wickets. It had taken him fewer Tests, 56, than Gibbs, and had it not been for the years lost to serious back injury and World Series Cricket, he might have had 400 or more.

Another record to fall in 1981-82 was Sir Gary Sobers' aggregate of 8,032 runs in Tests. In New Delhi, Geoffrey Boycott, making his 107th appearance for England – and his first tour of India – bettered that figure and at Calcutta increased it to 8,114 before going off to play golf while his team-mates spent the day in the field watching Gavaskar advance inexorably towards their enigmatic opener's record. Soon afterwards, with two Tests of the series still to be played, Boycott returned to England, feeling 'pretty tired', and it was generally agreed that his Test career had come to an end. His decision to tour South Africa several months later with a group of English players, and the subsequent three-year Test ban on those involved, virtually ensured he would never play for England again.

It was fitting that the last meeting, at Test level, between Lillee and Boycott saw them emerge with honours even. In his first innings of the sixth Test against the 1981 Australians, Boycott scored 137 before Yallop magnificently caught him in the gully off Lillee. In the second innings Lillee had him lbw, fourth ball, for nought. Both men were past their peak, they never met when either was at his, but such was the reputation, the aura, surrounding them that there was a special drama every time the smoothly geared fast bowler moved in to bowl to that most resolute of English batsmen.

In the summer of 1981 the pair had renewed acquaintance at Trent Bridge, where the moisture and cloud were much in Lillee's favour. Though still overcoming the debilitating effects of bronchial congestion, he took eight wickets as England were bowled out for 185 and 125. Alderman, a surprise selection ahead of Thomson for the tour, captured nine wickets with his lively fast-medium seam and swing, and the Australian fielding recalled the heady days of the mid-1970s. England's catching, on the other hand, was poor: in Australia's first innings of 179 at least six chances went to ground. For the fourth successive tour there was a Chappell in the Australian side, this time Trevor, a younger brother of Ian and Greg. And it was he who, on the first Sunday of Test cricket in England, hit the winning run that put Australia one-up in the series. Greg Chappell had declined to tour and so the captaincy had reverted to Hughes.

England's captaincy had remained with Botham, although only on a tenuous Test-at-a-time basis. At Trent Bridge, where he was top-scorer with 33 in England's second innings, he had done enough to retain it for Lord's, but his bowling, in conditions that should have suited him, was discouragingly ineffective. He claimed that the captaincy was not affecting his game, but when he failed to score in either innings of the second Test the main talking-point was whether he should even be selected for the third Test, let alone captain the side. He ended speculation about the latter issue by tendering his resignation on the last day of what had been a moribund Lord's Test from the time that the umpires, on Saturday evening, misread the playing conditions. England's 311 was capably matched by Australia's 345; in the second innings Boycott, playing in his 100th Test, and Gower kept the Australians in the field long enough to secure a draw. There was a moment, with Australia 17 for three, when it looked as if England might snatch a surprise victory, but Wood and Chappell made sure there would be no last-minute reprieve for Botham.

For the third Test, at Headingley, Botham returned to the ranks and Brearley came back as captain, although the changes seemed insignificant when England, in reply to Australia's 401 for nine, crumbled to 174 before Lillee, Alderman and Lawson. The latter, following up his eight wickets at Lord's, looked to be another fine prospect for Australia. The only bright spot for England was Botham's six wickets in Australia's innings and his swiftly struck half-century before becoming Marsh's record 264th Test dismissal. Gloom and despondency continued as England, following on 227 behind, were reduced to 135 for seven by Monday afternoon; at which stage Dilley, blond curls encaptured within a helmet, walked out to pass the time of day with Botham.

The rest is history. Botham rocketed to a thunderous 149 to make Australia bat again, Willis bowled as if reborn, Brearley conjured and cajoled, suddenly the catches were held and England won on the final afternoon by 18 runs. At Edgbaston, England won by 29 runs, thanks to one of Botham's extraordinary five-wicket deciders; at Old Trafford it was Botham with the bat once more, hitting a hundred off 86 balls, and Brearley retained the Ashes he first won in 1967. Botham had played in his first Test then. Now he stood on the verge of the double 'double' of 2,000 runs and 200 wickets in Tests. The wickets he claimed in the drawn sixth Test at The Oval, the runs had to wait until India.

For the Australians there was only the satisfaction of personal achievements: Alderman's record 42 wickets for an Anglo-Australian series, Marsh's wicket-keeping record and Border's brave unbeaten hundreds at Old Trafford and The Oval with a broken finger, Wellham's début hundred at The Oval. However, the return of Greg Chappell as captain for the three series against Pakistan, West Indies and New Zealand would strengthen the side, even though his batting form was to be uncharacteristically erratic.

With Brearley unavailable, England brought in Fletcher as captain for their tour of India and Sri Lanka. India also recalled a player who, like Fletcher, had been out of Test cricket since 1977: all-rounder Madan Lal, who claimed an early wicket in the first Test at Bombay when he bowled Gooch. England – Botham and Dilley in particular – had already dismissed India for 179, and while Boycott and Tavaré were slowly accumulating runs a first-innings lead looked probable. Then nine wickets fell for 71, with the bespectacled Doshi taking five for 39 by exploiting the English batsmen's penchant for the sweep. Often an ill-advised stroke, the sweep became positively lethal when

ventured before an Indian umpire – or so it appeared from the reaction of certain players to their dismissal. Even the England captain was to swipe down the stumps in anger before the series was over.

Botham, who took five more wickets in the second innings, had bowled England into a winning position when India were 157 for eight, but they were frustrated by the 'Indian Botham'. With amazing hitting on an uncertain wicket, Kapil Dev struck 46 from 51 balls; and when England batted, needing 241 with almost two days in which to score them, he and Madan Lal took five wickets each as England crashed to 102, their lowest-ever score in India.

England's disastrous batting not only lost them the Test; it was to cost them the series, for the remaining five matches were dreary, drawn affairs. Indeed, in four of them the first innings did not finish until the fifth day, though this was hardly surprising when India's spin bowlers could slow the over-rate to as few as 12, even 10, overs an hour. Gavaskar, with a win under his belt, was content to let Fletcher take the risks, but the England captain seemed to look no further than a draw. Had his fielders been less profligate he might occasionally have established a foothold, especially in Madras where Allott alone had three or four catches dropped off his bowling.

Gower, Gooch, a century-maker in Madras, and Botham at least attempted to entertain the vast crowds with some stroke-play, and Botham's hundred in the final Test was the well-merited culmination of a series of responsible batting. Yet even then he was overshadowed by Kapil Dev who, with the pressure off, blitzed a hundred in 83 balls – faster than either of Botham's centuries against the Australians the previous English summer. Other three-figure innings, such as Boycott's 105 and Tavaré's 149 in New Delhi, Gavaskar's eleven-and-three-quarter-hours 172 in Bangalore, Viswanath's 222 and Yashpal Sharma's 140 in Madras, were slowly gathered sandbags for the trenches in the war of attrition.

From India, England travelled on to Colombo where, for a time, they were in danger of a humiliating defeat but came back through Underwood, Emburey, Tavaré and Gower to win Sri Lanka's first-ever Test match. Several weeks later, in Pakistan, the Sri Lankans endured their inaugural Test series, going down 2-0 in a three-Test rubber

which attracted more notice for the refusal of some senior Pakistan cricketers to play under Javed Miandad than for noteworthy performances by the Test newcomers. The recalcitrant Pakistanis returned for the final Test only after the announcement that Javed would not lead his country on their forthcoming tour of England.

The seeds of this particular Pakistani mutiny had been sown in Australia, where Pakistan were well beaten in the first two Tests but saved some face with an innings victory in the third Test. The most encouraging feature of this series was the success of Australia's off-spinner Yardley, who took 18 wickets in the three Tests and later captured another 33 against West Indies and New Zealand. Less pleasing was Lillee's kicking of Javed during the first Test, a nasty flash of temper which could have marred a momentous season for the great bowler. Fortunately this misdemeanour was forgiven (if not forgotten) by the time Lillee took 10 wickets in the first Test against West Indies to overtake Gibbs' world record and help win the match for Australia. Dyson's resistance at Sydney prevented West Indies from squaring the series, but there was no stopping Holding, Roberts and Garner at Adelaide, where Gomes hit his second hundred of the series and West Indies won by five wickets.

Australia then went to New Zealand, by way of compensation for that country's cancelled tour of the West Indies. After the first Test had been washed out, New Zealand won at Auckland, helped by Edgar's 161 and Hadlee's pace bowling, but Australia levelled the series at Christchurch, where Greg Chappell showed a welcome return to form with 176 and Thomson, Lillee and Alderman made the Kiwis follow on. It was, for Australia, a satisfactory end to a year that had begun so promisingly at Trent Bridge and had then been wrested from their control by Botham's freed spirit. They could look ahead with confidence more than apprehension to the following season's Ashes series, whereas England, rebuilding, had to replace not only Boycott but also Gooch, likewise a casualty of the South African adventure. Both countries were looking for young fast bowlers to replace their ageing stars, but if none was forthcoming, who would bemoan a spin bowler heralding the start of another decade of Test cricket?

Woolmer is caught by Wood off Lillee (*right*), the first of two noughts for him in the match.

A hopelessly out of touch Botham is bowled by Alderman for 1 (*below*).

Lillee had lost none of his touch. Slower, perhaps, but no less dangerous.

Gatting was the best of the England batsmen, with 52 in the first innings.

Boycott opens the innings with Gooch, it was his 100th Test appearance for England.

Gower had his fortunate moments. The Australian slips (*top*) watch as one edge flies out of reach above them – from left Marsh, Dyson, Alderman, Border and Wood each register their own dismay. Gower just gets home (*left*), although it was a very close thing. Botham (*above*) made 0 in each innings – here Lawson gets him lbw. Having lost the first Test and drawn the second, and with his personal performances at an all time low, he resigned the captaincy. One wondered if he should be picked for the side for the next Test.

201

Headingley lived up to its reputation, and the Yorkshire crowd, well versed in the technique of keeping dry, wait patiently. Hughes (*below*) has a nasty moment against Willis but must have felt well satisfied when England were 133 for seven in their second innings, still 92 runs behind Australia, and facing defeat by an innings. The odds against an England win were quoted at 500-1. As Dilley came to join Botham, the latter said, ''You don't feel like hanging around here for a day, do you ? Let's give it some humpety.'' And humpety they did. Botham played with a mixture of the watchful and the outrageous in what must be one of the most spectacular Test innings of all time. At close of play he was 145 not out.

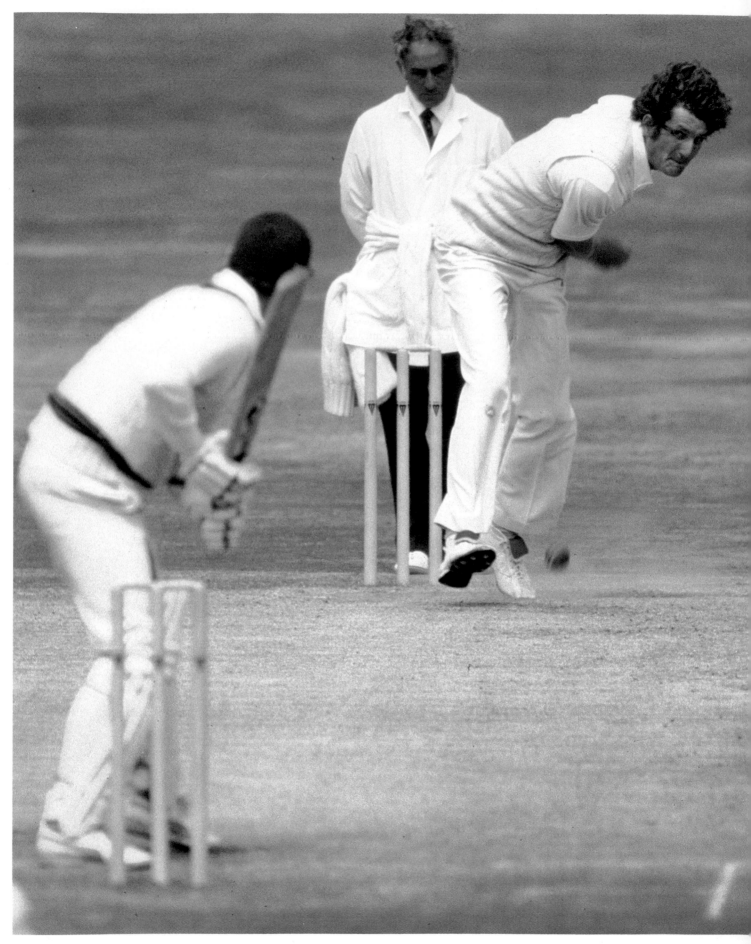

Willis bowled as one inspired, perhaps by Brearley. His eight wickets cost 43 runs as Australia collapsed in disarray.

Australia started well enough, being 56 for 1 at one stage, but by the time Taylor caught Dyson (his 1,270th catch) they were 68-6.

Australia all out for 111, lose by 18 runs. Botham and Taylor run the gauntlet and just make it to the safety of the dressing-room.

Following their victory at Headingley, England won again in only slightly less improbable circumstances. Australia needed only 151 to win in their second innings and these two wickets were vital; Border (*above*) is caught by Gatting, and Yallop by Botham (*below left*), both off Emburey. Botham, who had failed with the bat (usually an ominous sign for his opponents), then took the last five wickets for one run in 26 balls. Last man Alderman goes for 0 (*below right*) and an England crowd enjoy the sunshine as well as the victory (*facing page*).

After Allott, playing in his first Test, and Willis had helped England to 231 they took four quick wickets. Here Hughes is lbw to Willis.

Later Willis takes his third wicket in the same over, as Botham catches Yallop at third slip (*above*). Australia never recovered and were all out for 130. As England's second innings became more and more lifeless, their advantage seemed to slip away until Botham reappeared and played an innings to rank with that at Headingley. He drives Lillee for 4 (*facing page*) during his 118, scored in 123 minutes off only 102 balls. He hit six sixes and thirteen fours and 90 of his runs came off 49 deliveries with the new ball.

Paul Allott, making his Test debut on his home ground, could count on the punster's support (*lower left*). Old Trafford was packed for each of the first four days (*top left*). Australia faced an uphill struggle having been set 506 to win, but in this topsy-turvy series it looked for a time as if they might make it, thanks to the efforts of Graham Yallop (*above*) with 114 and Allan Border, who batted with a broken finger for 123 not out (*right*). In the event the target was out of reach and when Marsh was out for 47, Australia were soon dismissed for 402. England retained the Ashes, a result that seemed totally impossible less than a month before, at about 4.15pm on the 20th July.

That's out. Botham shows Hughes the evidence that he had dislodged a bail while hooking.

Yallop and Lillee celebrate, after Yallop had caught Boycott in the gully.

Botham holds the ball safely (*left*) after catching Marsh off Willis. Perhaps off Tavaré would be a more accurate description, since the ball had rebounded from Tavaré before Botham took the catch.

Brearley (*left*), says farewell to Test cricket with a half century and in this symbolic tableau sends Hughes into retreat. Botham reached a fresh land-mark with his 200th Test wicket. Marsh (*above*) skies him to the mid wicket boundary where Gatting safely made the catch, leaving the exceptionally talented all-rounder to salute his achievement (*below*).

215

Geoff Boycott gathered another 63 runs on his way to the record he eventually achieved in Delhi (*above*). A great slip catch (*below*) as Tavaré catches Vengsarkar. As the match progressed the fire crackers became more violent (*above, centre*). Ian Botham scores his 2,000th Test run (*far right*) and joins Sir Garfield Sobers and Richie Benaud with 2,000 runs and 200 wickets in Tests. Tavaré is caught by Gavaskar off Kapil Dev (*below right*) and England begin their slide into defeat – the only result in the series.

Pre-Christmas, and with the series decided, the attendance at the MCG was woeful (*above*). A total of 33,768 for the match.

Marsh can hardly hide his enthusiasm as he successfully appeals for lbw. against Miandad (*left*).

Dennis Lillee, who was shortly to become the leading wicket-taker in Test matches, breaking Gibbs' record at Melbourne, himself congratulates Imran Khan, who, when he dismissed Marsh, became Pakistan's top wicket-taker (*right*).

Key to Centenary Test group on page 184-185

1 F. J. Bryant (Australian Cricket Board) 2 T. C. J. Caldwell (ACB) 3 L. V. Maddocks 4 A. N. Connolly

5 M. H. N. Walker 6 A. E. Moss 7 P. E. Richardson 8 C. R. Ingamells (ACB) 9 K. R. Stackpole 10 R. A. L. Massie

11 R. B. Simpson 12 R. T. Simpson 13 W. M. Lawry 14 A. Turner 15 R. Tattersall 16 R. A. Gaunt

17 M. J. McInnes (ACB) 18 A. W. Walsh (ACB) 19 J. W. Gleeson 20 A. C. Smith 21 G. B. Hole 22 D. L. Richards (ACB)

23 D. A. Allen 24 R. M. Prideaux 25 H. W. H. Rigg (ACB) 26 R. Subba Row 27 T. R. Veivers 28 F. J. Titmus

29 F. W. C. Bennett (ACB) 30 K. D. Mackay ... ... artwright 32 R. Edwards 33 J. T. Murray 34 W. Watson

35 R. M. Cowper 36 C. S. Serjeant 37 J. S. ... ... J. K. Smith 38 J. M. Parks 40 C. C. McDonald

41 B. L. D'Oliveira 42 A. S. M. Oakman 43 J. A. Flavell 44 J. A. Ledward (ACB) 45 L. J. Coldwell

46 R. Benaud 47 I. R. Redpath 48 G. R. A. Langley 49 P. H. Edmonds 50 G. A. R. Lock 51 F. E. Rumsey

52 J. H. de Courcy 53 K. V. Andrew 54 R. B. McCosker 55 H. B. Taber 56 J. H. Hampshire 57 F. M. Misson

58 T. W. Graveney 59 A. K. Davidson 60 K. D. Walters 61 G. D. McKenzie 62 P. J. Loader 63 E. W. Freeman

64 G. D. Watson 65 G. E. Corling 66 A. J. W. McIntyre 67 D. B. Close 68 G. J. Gilmour 69 I. M. Chappell

70 F. H. Tyson 71 R. Illingworth 72 D. J. Colley 73 J. B. Statham 74 K. Taylor 75 P. H. Parfitt

76 R. Appleyard 77 P. J. Sharpe 78 C. G. Howard (MCC) 79 I. J. Jones 80 E. R. Dexter 81 A. R. Barnes (ACB)

82 I. D. Craig 83 C. S. Elliott (TCCB) 84 V. J. W. M. Lawrence (MCC) 85 K. F. Barrington 86 J. H. Wardle

87 W. E. Bowes 88 J. G. Dewes 89 A. G. Chipperfield 90 C. J. Barnett 91 T. G. Evans 92 E. W. Clark

93 J. A. Young 94 W. Voce 95 J. C. Laker 96 Sir L. Hutton 97 E. R. H. Toshack 98 E. L. McCormick

99 W. A. Johnston 100 K. E. Rigg 101 A. R. Morris 102 D. T. Ring 103 F. R. Brown 104 S. J. E. Loxton

105 K. R. Miller 106 D. V. P. Wright 107 A. V. Bedser 108 K. Cranston 109 M. G. Waite 110 C. Washbrook

111 C. L. Badcock 112 N. W. D. Yardley 113 A. L. Hassett 114 H. E. Dollery 115 W. A. Brown 116 J. T. Ikin

117 L. G. James (MCC) 118 W. E. Hollies 119 J. A. Bailey (MCC Secretary) 120 A. R. Border 121 J. Dyson

122 G. Dymock 123 R. J. Bright 124 B. M. Laird 125 G. M. Wood 126 G. N. Yallop 127 K. J. Hughes

128 R. W. Marsh 129 L. S. Pascoe 130 J. R. Thomson 131 A. A. Mallett 132 D. K. Lillee 133 P. M. Lush (TCCB)

134 J. R. Stephenson (MCC) 135 D. B. Carr (TCCB Secretary) 136 D. J. Constant (umpire) 137 P. Willey

138 J. Emburey 139 C. W. J. Athey 140 R. D. Jackman 141 D. L. Bairstow 142 M. W. Gatting 143 C. M. Old

144 M. Hendrick 145 G. Boycott 146 G. A. Gooch 147 D. I. Gower 148 H. D. Bird (umpire) 149 W. J. O'Reilly

150 L. S. Darling 151 E. L. a'Beckett 152 W. H. Ponsford 153 A. Sandham 154 R. C. Steele (ACB)

155 P. B. H. May 156 G. S. Chappell 157 S. C. Griffith (MCC President) 158 I. T. Botham

159 R. J. Parish (ACB Chairman) 160 F. G. Mann (TCCB Chairman) 161 H. S. T. L. Hendry 162 G. O. B. Allen

163 R. E. S. Wyatt 164 P. G. H. Fender

Abdul Qadir (1977/78) 122
Abid Ali, S (1974) 47
Adelaide
  1979/80, Australia v. West Indies 154, 166-7
Alderman, Terry (1981) 196, 197, 198, 201, 206
Ali, Inshan (1973) 29
Alley, Mr Bill (umpire) 85
Allot, Paul (1981) 197, 208, 211
Amarnath, Mohinder (1978) 131, 145
Amiss, Dennis (1972) 13; (1973) 30, 31, 33; (1974) 44, 49, 55; (1975) 65; (1976) 85, 96; (1977) 110
Angelow, Michael 71
Arlott, John (broadcaster) 12, 64, 187
Arnold, Geoff (1972) 12, 14; (1973) 30, 31, 33, 34, 35; (1974) 44, 49; (1975) 64
Asif Iqbal (1972) 13
Australia
  v. England, 1972, 1975, 1977, 1980, 1981 see England
  v. England, 1974/75 44; *2nd Test* Perth 56-7; *3rd Test* Melbourne 58-9; *4th Test* Sydney 60-3
  v. England, 1977 84; *Centenary Test* Melbourne 104-9
  v. England, 1978/79 130; *2nd Test* Perth 148-9; *3rd Test* Melbourne 150-1; *4th Test* Sydney 152-3
  v. England, 1979/80 154; *2nd Test* Sydney 164-5; *3rd Test* Melbourne 168-9
  v. Pakistan, 1981 196; *3rd Test* Melbourne 218-19
  v. West Indies, 1973, 1978 see West Indies
  v. West Indies, 1975/76 64; *1st Test* Brisbane 76-7; *2nd Test* Perth 78-9; *3rd Test* Melbourne 80-1; *4th Test* Sydney 82-3
  v. West Indies, 1979/80 154; *3rd Test* Adelaide 166-7
Australian Cricket Board 1975, TV rights negotiations 64

Bacchus, Faoud (1978) 131; (1980) 179, 180
Bailey, Trevor (1973) 31
Bairstow, David (1979) 161; (1980) 187
Balderstone, Chris (1976) 93, 97
Barrington, Ken 172, 194
Bedi, Bishan (1972) 13; (1974) 44, 50; (1975) 65; (1976/77) 85, 98; (1978) 111, 130, 147; (1979) 154, 161
Benaud, Richie 216
Bird, Mr Dickie (umpire) 136
Bombay
  1980, India v. England 154, 170-1
  1981/82, India v. England 196, 216-17
Border, Allan (1979) 155; (1981) 197, 201, 206, 211
Botham, Ian (1977) 111, 117, 119; (1978) 111, 130, 132, 134, 135, 143; (1978/79) 131, 149; (1979) 154, 155, 159, 160, 161; (1979/80) 164, 169; (1980) 170, 171, 173, 178; (1981) 196, 198, 201, 202, 205, 206, 208, 213, 215; (1981/82) 197, 216
Bowling, action photographs 9, 10-11

Boyce, Keith (1972) 13; (1973) 30, 31
Boycott, Geoff (1972) 12, 13, 14, 19; (1973) 30, 31, 35, 39; (1974) 44, 47; (1975) 64; (1977) 110, 111, 116, 119; (1978) 122, 130, 140; (1978/79) 149, 151, 154, 155, 156; (1980) 173, 177, 180, 187; (1981) 192, 200; (1981/82) 216
Bracewell, Brendon (1978) 140
Bradman, Sir Donald 30, 104
Brearley, Mike (1976/77) 85, 98, 102; (1977) 104, 110, 113, 114; (1977/78) 111, 122; (1978) 130, 131, 134; (1978/79) 131, 153; (1979) 154, 155, 159; (1981) 197, 204, 215
Bridgetown
  1973, West Indies v. Australia 12, 26-7
  1978, West Indies v. Australia 110, 126-7
  1981, West Indies v. England 172, 192-5
Brisbane
  1975/76, Australia v. West Indies 64, 76-7
Burgess, Mark (1973) 30; (1978) 138, 143

Calcutta
  1976/77, India v. England 84, 98-101
Chandrasekhar, B.S. (1972) 13; (1974) 44, 47; (1976/77) 98; (1978) 111, 127; (1979) 154
Chappell, Greg (1972) 12, 13, 18, 19, 24; (1973) 27, 31; (1974/75) 45, 63; (1975) 65, 66, 67; (1975/76) 76, 84, 85; (1977) 104, 110, 113, 115, 117; (1979/80) 155, 164; (1981) 196, 197
Chappell, Ian (1972) 13, 24; (1973) 31; (1974) 45; (1975) 64, 65, 67, 72; (1975/76) 76, 77, 79, 80, 82; (1976) 84, 85; (1979/80) 155, 164; (1980) 172
Chappell, Trevor (1981) 196
Chatfield, Ewan (1974) 45
Chauhan, Chetan (1979) 154, 155; (1980) 172
Clark, Wayne (1977) 111
Clarke, Sylvester (1980) 172
Close, Brian (1976) 84, 85, 88, 89
Collinge, Richard (1978) 111
Congdon, Bevan (1973) 30, 33, 34
Cosier, Gary (1975/76) 80; (1977) 109; (1978) 127
Cowdrey, Colin (1974) 45; (1974/75) 56, 58
Croft, Colin (1976/77) 85; (1978) 124; (1979/80) 154, 167; (1980) 173, 180; (1981) 190

Daniel, Wayne (1976) 84, 85
Denness, Mike (1972) 13; (1973) 31; (1974) 44, 45, 47, 49; (1975) 64, 66, 70
Dilley, Graham (1980) 179; (1981) 192, 197, 202
D'Oliveira, Basil (1972) 13, 15, 20, 24
Doshi, Dilip (1980) 172; (1981/82) 197
Downton, Paul (1981) 173
Dymock, Geoff (1979) 155
Dyson, John (1981) 197, 201

Edgar, Bruce (1978) 138; (1981) 197
Edgbaston
  1973, England v. West Indies 30, 38-9
  1974, England v. India 44, 50

1975, England v. Australia 64, 66-9
1978, England v. Pakistan 130, 132-3
1979, England v. India 154, 156-7
1981, England v. Australia 196, 204-7
Edmonds, Phil (1975) 65, 72; (1978) 138
Edrich, Bill (1938) 30
Edrich, John (1972) 12; (1974) 44, 45, 47; (1975) 65, 67, 71; (1976) 84, 89
Edwards, Ross (1972) 13, 19, 21; (1973) 29; (1974) 45; (1975) 64, 65, 67, 70, 72; (1978) 140
Emburey, John (1978/79) 131, 153; (1981/82) 197, 206
Engineer, Farokh (1972) 13; (1974) 49
England
  v. Australia, 1972 12; *1st Test* Old Trafford 14-17; *2nd Test* Lord's 18-19; *3rd Test* Trent Bridge 20-1; *4th Test* Headingley 22-3; *5th Test* The Oval 24-5
  v. Australia, 1974/75, 1977, 1978/79, 1979/80 see Australia
  v. Australia, 1975 64; *1st Test* Edgbaston 66-9; *2nd Test* Lord's 70-1; *3rd Test* Headingley 72-3; *4th Test* The Oval 74-5
  v. Australia, 1977 110; *1st Test* Lord's 112-13; *2nd Test* Old Trafford 114-15; *3rd Test* Trent Bridge 116-17; *4th Test* Headingley 118-19; *5th Test* The Oval 119-21
  v. Australia, 1980 172; *Centenary Test* Lord's 184-7
  v. Australia, 1981 196; *1st Test* Trent Bridge 198-9; *2nd Test* Lord's 200-1; *3rd Test* Headingley 202-3; *4th Test* Edgbaston 204-7; *5th Test* Old Trafford 208-11; *6th Test* The Oval 212-15
  v. India, 1976/77, 1980, 1981/82 see India
  v. India, 1974 44; *1st Test* Old Trafford 46-7; *2nd Test* Lord's 48-9; *3rd Test* Edgbaston 50
  v. India, 1979 154; *1st Test* Edgbaston 156-7; *2nd Test* Lord's 158-9; *3rd Test* Headingley 160; *4th Test* The Oval 161-3
  v. New Zealand, 1973 30; *1st Test* Trent Bridge 32-3; *2nd Test* Lord's 34; *3rd Test* Headingley 35
  v. New Zealand, 1978 130; *1st Test* The Oval 136-9; *2nd Test* Trent Bridge 140-1; *3rd Test* Lord's 142-3
  v. Pakistan, 1974 44; *1st Test* Headingley 51; *2nd Test* Lord's 52-3; *3rd Test* The Oval 54-5
  v. Pakistan, 1977/78 see Pakistan
  v. Pakistan, 1978 130; *1st Test* Edgbaston 132-3; *2nd Test* Lord's 134-5; *3rd Test* Headingley
  v. West Indies, 1973 30; *1st Test* The Oval 36-7; *2nd Test* Edgbaston 38-9; *3rd Test* Lord's 40-3
  v. West Indies, 1976 84; *1st Test* Trent Bridge 86-7; *2nd Test* Lord's 88-9; *3rd Test* Old Trafford 89-91; *4th Test* Headingley 92-3; *5th Test* The Oval 94-7
  v. West Indies, 1980 172; *1st Test* Trent Bridge 174-5; *2nd Test* Lord's 176-7;

3rd Test Old Trafford 178-9; *4th Test*
  The Oval 180-1; *5th Test* Headingley
  182-3
  v. West Indies, 1981 *see* West Indies

Fagg, Mr Arthur (umpire) 31, 39
Fishwick, Herbert (photographer) 8
Fletcher, Keith (1972) 13; (1973) 30, 31, 34,
  40; (1974) 44, 45, 55; (1974/75) 61, 64,
  65; (1977) 106; (1981) 197
Fredericks, Roy (1973) 38; (1975/76) 65,
  79; (1976) 84, 93, 94
Francis, Bruce (1972) 19

Gaekwad, Anshuman (1978/79) 131
Garner, Joel (1976) 85; (1978) 124, 126,
  128; (1979) 154; (1979/80) 167; (1980)
  182; (1981) 192, 197
Gatting, Mike (1980) 187; (1981) 199,
  206, 215
Gavaskar, Sunil (1974) 47; (1976/77) 85;
  (1978) 111, 130, 131, 145, 147; (1979)
  154, 156, 159, 162; (1980) 170, 172;
  (1981/82) 197, 216
Georgetown
  1981, West Indies v. England 172, 191
Ghavri, Karsan (1978) 131; (1979) 154
Gibbs, Lance (1972) 13; (1973) 31;
  (1975/76) 76, 80; (1981) 196
Gilmour, Gary (1975/76) 65, 76; (1977) 104
Gleeson, John (1972) 12, 19
Gomes, Larry (1978) 111; (1981) 197
Gooch, Graham (1975) 65, 66; (1978/79)
  131; (1979/80) 154, 169; (1980) 155, 173,
  177, 179; (1981) 191, 192, 197, 200
Gower, David (1978) 130, 132, 138;
  (1978/79) 131, 149; (1979) 154, 156;
  (1980) 155, 187; (1981) 173, 196, 201;
  (1981/82) 197
Greenidge, Gordon (1974) 45; (1975/76)
  76; (1976) 84, 85, 88, 89, 93, 94;
  (1978) 127, 129; (1980) 181
Greig, Tony 11; (1972) 12, 13, 15; (1973)
  30, 31, 33; (1974) 45, 47, 49; (1974/75)
  63; (1975) 64, 65, 66, 70, 74; (1976) 84,
  85, 86, 88, 93, 96; (1977) 98, 102, 104,
  110, 112, 114; (1979/80) 164

Hadlee, Dayle (1973) 30, 31; (1976/77) 85;
  (1978) 137, 143
Hadlee, Richard (1973) 31; (1978) 111;
  (1980) 155; (1981) 197
Hammond, John (1972) 13
Hayes, Frank (1973) 31, 36
Haynes, Desmond (1980) 173, 174, 176, 182
Headingley
  1972, England v. Australia 12, 22-3
  1973, England v. New Zealand 30, 35
  1974, England v. Pakistan 44, 51
  1975, England v. Australia 64, 72-3
  1976, England v. West Indies 84, 92-3
  1977, England v. Australia 110, 118-19
  1978, England v. Pakistan 130
  1979, England v. India 154, 160
  1980, England v. West Indies 172, 182-3
  1981, England v. Australia 196, 202-3
Headley, Ron (1973) 31

Hendrick, Mike (1978) 131, 143; (1979)
  157; (1980) 186
Higgs, Jim (1978) 127; (1978/79) 153
Hilditch, Andrew (1978) 131
Hogg, Rodney (1978/79) 131, 151
Holder, Vanburn (1973) 30, 39; (1976) 84;
  (1978) 111
Holding, Michael 8, 9; (1975) 65; (1976)
  84, 85, 89, 96, 97; (1979/80) 154, 167,
  172; (1981) 192, 197
Hookes, David (1977) 106
Howarth, Geoff (1978) 111, 138, 143
Hughes, Kim (1977) 110; (1979/80) 155,
  167, 169; (1980) 172, 173, 186;
  (1981) 196, 202, 208, 215

Illingworth, Ray (1972) 12, 13, 23;
  (1973) 30, 31, 38; (1974/75) 63
Imran Khan (1976/77) 85; (1977/78) 111;
  (1981) 218
India
  v. England, 1974 *see* England
  v. England 1976/77 84; *2nd Test* Calcutta
    98-101; *3rd Test* Madras 102-3
  v. England, 1980 154; *Jubilee Test*
    Bombay 170-1
  v. England, 1981/82 196; *1st Test*
    Bombay 216-17
  v. Pakistan, 1978 *see* Pakistan
Intikhab Alam (1972) 13; (1974) 53
Inverarity, John (1972) 23
Iqbal Qasim (1978) 130, 132

Jackman, Robin 10; (1980) 172;
  (1981) 191, 192
Javed Miandad (1976/77) 85; (1978) 131,
  134, 145; (1981) 197, 218
Jones, Alderman Clem 45, 65
Julien, Bernard (1973) 30, 31, 40;
  (1975/76) 79
Jumadeen, Raphick (1976) 84; (1978) 111

Kallicharran, Alvin (1973) 28, 31, 36, 38;
  (1978) 131; (1980) 181, 182
Kanhai, Rohan (1972) 13; (1973) 30, 31
Kapil Dev (1978) 131; (1979) 154, 155;
  (1980) 172; (1981/82) 197, 216
Karachi
  1977/78, Pakistan v. England 110, 122-3
King Dial (Barbados personality) 194
Kirmani, Syed (1976/77) 98
Knott, Alan (1972) 13, 15, 20, 23; (1973)
  35, 38; (1974) 45, 47, 49; (1975) 58, 64;
  (1976) 84, 85, 93, 96; (1977) 109, 110,
  111, 117, 119

Lahore
  1978, Pakistan v. India 130, 144-7
Lawson, Geoff (1981) 196-7, 201
Lever, John 8; (1975) 70; (1976/77) 102
Lever, Peter (1974) 45; (1975) 64, 65;
  (1976/77) 85
Lewis, Tony (1972) 13
Lillee, Dennis, action photographs, bowling
  9-10; (1972) 12, 13, 14, 19, 20; (1973) 31;
  (1974/75) 45, 56, 58, 61, 63; (1975) 64, 65,

67, 70, 74; (1976) 76, 79, 84, 85;
  (1979/80) 155; (1980) 173, 187; (1981)
  196, 197, 198, 199, 208, 213, 218
Lloyd, Clive (1972) 13; (1973) 31, 38;
  (1974) 45; (1975/76) 65, 79, 82; (1977)
  111; (1979/80) 167, 173, 179; (1981) 194
Lloyd, David (1974) 44, 50, 51, 52, 53;
  (1974/75) 56, 61
Lord's
  1972, England v. Australia 12, 18-19
  1973, England v. New Zealand 30, 34
  1973, England v. West Indies 30, 40-3
  1974, England v. India 44, 48-9
  1974, England v. Pakistan 44, 52-3
  1975, England v. Australia 64, 70-1
  1976, England v. West Indies 84, 88-9
  1977, England v. Australia 110, 112-13
  1978, England v. Pakistan 130, 134-5
  1978, England v. New Zealand 130, 142-3
  1979, England v. India 154, 158-9
  1980, England v. West Indies 172, 176-7
  1980, England v. Australia 172, 184-7
  1981, England v. Australia 196, 200-1
Lovitt, Ron (photographer) 8
Luckhurst, Brian (1972) 15, 20

McCosker, Rick (1975) 65, 67, 74;
  (1977) 106
Maclean, John (1978/79) 149
Madan Lal (1976/77) 98; (1981) 197
Madras
  1976/77, India v. England 84, 102-3
Majid Khan (1974) 51, 52; (1977/78) 111
Mallett, Ashley (1972) 13, 24; (1974/75)
  63, 67; (1976/77) 85
Marsh, Rodney (1972) 12, 15, 19, 23;
  (1973) 28; (1974/75) 58, 63; (1975) 65,
  66, 67; (1975/76) 82; (1977) 104, 106,
  110, 117, 119; (1979/80) 169;
  (1981) 197, 201, 211, 213, 215, 218
Massie, Bob (1972) 12, 13, 19, 20
Mattis, Everton (1981) 188
Melbourne
  1974/75, Australia v. England 44, 58-9
  1975/76, Australia v. West Indies 64, 80-1
  1977, Australia v. England 84, 104-9
  1978/79, Australia v. England 130, 150-1
  1979/80, Australia v. England 154, 168-9
  1981, Australia v. Pakistan 196, 218-19
Miller, Geoff (1978) 134; (1978/79) 131,
  153; (1979) 154
Mohsin Khan (1978) 136
Mudassar Nazar (1977/78) 111, 122
Murray, Deryck (1973) 39; (1975/76) 82;
  (1976) 88, 93; (1979/80) 167; (1981) 190
Mushtaq Mohammad (1972) 13; (1977) 85;
  (1977/78) 111

New Zealand
  v. England, 1973, 1978 *see* England

Oakman, Alan (1973) 39
O'Keeffe, Kerry (1977) 104, 109, 113
Old, Chris (1973) 30, 38; (1974) 44, 49, 55;
  (1975) 64; (1977) 104; (1978) 130, 132;
  (1980) 187
Old Trafford

1972, England v. Australia 12, 14-17
1974, England v. India 44, 46-7
1976, England v. West Indies 84, 89-91
1977, England v. Australia 110, 114-15
1980, England v. West Indies 172, 178-9
1981, England v. Australia 196, 208-11
Oulds, Dennis (photographer) 8

Packer, Kerry 8, 11; TV rights proposal 64;
    WSC team, (1977) 85, 110, 111, 112, 131;
    success, (1979) 131
Padmore, Albert (1976) 84
Palmer, Mr Ken (umpire) 136
Pakistan
    v. Australia, 1981 *see* Australia
    v. England, 1974, *see* England
    v. England, 1977/78 110; *3rd Test*
        Karachi 122-3
    v. India 1978 130; *2nd Test* Lahore 144-7
    v. Sri Lanka *New Test Series* 197
Parfitt, Peter (1972) 20, 23
Parker, John (1973) 35
Parry, Derek (1978) 111
Pascoe, Len (1977) 110, 111, 112;
    (1980) 173, 187
Pataudi, Nawab of (1974) 45
Patil, Sandeep (1980) 172
Perth
    1974/75, Australia v. England 44, 56-7
    1975/76, Australia v. West Indies 64, 78-9
    1978/79, Australia v. England 130, 148-9
Petherick, Peter (1976/77) 85
Photography, Test cricket 8-11
Piper, Eric (photographer) (1974) 49
Pollard, Vic (1973) 30
Port of Spain
    1973, West Indies v. Australia 12, 28-9
    1978, West Indies v. Australia 110, 124-5
    1981, West Indies v. England 172, 188-90
Prasanna, E.A.S. (1974) 44

Radley, Clive (1978) 131
Randall, Derek (1977) 109, 110, 111, 116,
    119; (1978/79) 131, 153; (1979) 154, 156
Reddy, Bharath (1979) 157
Redpath, Ian (1972) 13; (1974) 45, 63;
    (1975) 65, 76; (1976/77) 85
Richards, Viv (1974) 45; (1975) 65;
    (1975/76) 76, 82; (1976) 84, 86, 93, 94;
    (1978) 127; (1980) 173, 176, 177, 178, 181;
    (1981) 192, 194
Roberts, Andy (1975) 65; (1975/76) 76, 77,
    79; (1976) 84-5, 86, 93; (1978/79) 124,
    154; (1979/80) 167, 173; (1981) 197
Robinson, Richie (1977) 113
Roope, Graham (1973) 33; (1978) 135
Rose, Brian (1980) 173, 187
Rowe, Lawrence (1973) 28; (1975/76) 77,
    80, 82
Ryder, Jack (1977) 104

Sadiq Mohammad (1972) 13; (1974) 52;
    (1978) 130, 132, 136
Saeed Ahmed (1972) 13
Sang Hue, Mr D (umpire) 31
Sarfraz Nawaz (1974) 51; (1978) 130,
    131, 147

Selvey, Mike (1976) 97
Serjeant, Craig (1978) 110, 111, 124
Shafiq Ahmed (1977/78) 122
Shastri, Ravi (1980) 172
Sheahan, Paul (1972) 13
Sikander Bakht (1978) 131, 132
Simpson, Bobby (1977) 111; (1978) 111,
    124, 127
Smith, A.C. 191
Smith, Mike (1972) 19
Snow, John (1972) 12, 13, 14, 19, 20;
    (1973) 30, 31, 33, 35, 36; (1975) 64;
    (1976) 84, 88; (1977) 110
Sobers, Sir Gary (1972) 13; (1973) 30,
    31, 40; (1981) 196, 216
Solkar, E.D. (1976/77) 98
Spectator violence 10, 31
Sponsorship of Test matches 131
Sri Lanka v. Pakistan
    1981/82 *New Test Series* 197
Stackpole, Keith (1972) 13, 14, 15;
    (1973) 29
Steele, David (1975) 64, 65; (1976) 88
Sydney
    1974/75, Australia v. England 44, 60-3
    1975/76, Australia v. West Indies 64, 82-3
    1978/79, Australia v. England 130, 152-3
    1979/80, Australia v. England 154, 164-5

Talat Ali (1978) 135
Taslim Arif (1980) 155
Tavaré, Chris (1981) 197, 213; (1981/82) 216
Taylor, Bob (1977/78) 122; (1978) 131, 135;
    (1979) 156; (1980) 170; (1981) 205
The Oval
    1972, England v. Australia 12, 24-5
    1973, England v. West Indies 30, 36-7
    1974, England v. Pakistan 44, 54-5
    1975, England v. Australia 64, 74-5
    1976, England v. West Indies 84, 94-7
    1977, England v. Australia 110, 119-21
    1978, England v. New Zealand 130, 136-9
    1979, England v. India 154, 161-3
    1980, England v. West Indies 172, 180-1
    1981, England v. Australia 196, 212-15
Thomas, Bernard (MCC physiotherapist)45
Thomson, Jeff (1973) 31; (1974) 45, 56, 58,
    61, 63; (1975) 64, 65, 67, 70; (1975/76)
    80, 82; (1976) 84, 85; (1977) 110, 111;
    (1978) 127, 131; (1979/80) 155; (1981) 197
Titmus, Freddie (1974/75) 58
Tolchard, Roger (1976/77) 85
Toohey, Peter (1978) 124
Trent Bridge
    1972, England v. Australia 12, 20-1
    1973, England v. New Zealand 30, 32-3
    1976, England v. West Indies 84, 86-7
    1977, England v. Australia 110, 116-17
    1978, England v. New Zealand 130, 140-1
    1980, England v. West Indies 172, 174-5
    1981, England v. Australia 196, 198-9
Trueman, Fred (1975/76) 80
Turner, Glenn (1973) 30, 31, 33; (1975) 67

Umpires, 1973, pressures increase 31
Underwood, Derek 9; (1972) 12-13, 23;
    (1973) 40; (1974) 45, 47, 52, 53, 55;
    (1975) 65; (1976) 84, 85, 89; (1976/77)

102, 104, 110, 115; (1979/80) 164;
    (1981) 197

Vandalism 65
Vengsarkar, Dilip (1978) 131; (1979) 155,
    159; (1981/82) 216
Venkataraghavan, S. (1974) 44; (1979) 155,
    161
Viswanath, Gundappa (1972) 13; (1974)
    47, 49; (1976/77) 102; (1979) 154, 159;
    (1980) 170; (1982/82) 197

Wadekar, Ajit (1974) 45
Wadsworth, Ken (1973) 30, 34
Walker, Max (1972) 13; (1973) 27, 28;
    (1974/75) 45, 63; (1975) 64, 65, 66, 67;
    (1975/76) 82; (1977) 106, 110, 114, 115
Walters, Doug (1972) 13, 23; (1973) 29;
    (1974) 45; (1974/75) 56; (1975) 65, 67,
    70, 72; (1977) 110, 117; (1980) 173
Wasim Bari (1974) 51; (1977/78) 123;
    (1978) 135
Wasim Raja (1974) 53; (1977/78) 111
Wellham, Dirk (1981) 197
West Indies
    v. Australia, 1973 12; *2nd Test*
        Bridgetown 26-7; *3rd Test* Port of
        Spain 28-9
    v. Australia, 1975/76, 1979/80 *see*
        Australia
    v. Australia, 1978 110; *1st Test* Port of
        Spain 124-5; *2nd Test* Bridgetown
        126-9
    v. England, 1973, 1976, 1980 *see* England
    v. England, 1981 172; *1st Test* Port of
        Spain 188-90; *2nd Test* Georgetown
        191; *3rd Test* Bridgetown 192-5
Wiener, Julian (1979/80) 167
Willey, Peter (1980) 180, 181
Williams, B. (1978) 111, 131
Willis, Bob (1972) 13; (1973) 31; (1974) 45;
    (1976) 84, 85, 93; (1977) 110, 122;
    (1978) 130, 132, 136, 143; (1979) 156;
    (1980) 173, 174, 180; (1981) 191, 197,
    202, 204, 208, 213
Wood, Barry (1972) 13; (1975) 64; (1978)
    111, 124; (1978/79) 149; (1980) 172-3,
    187; (1981) 196, 198, 201
Woolmer, Bob (1975) 64, 65; (1976) 96;
    (1977) 110, 113; (1981) 198
World Series Cricket 111, 131, 154, 196

Yadav, Shivlal (1980) 172
Yallop, Graham (1978) 111, 126; (1978/79)
    131; (1979) 155; (1980) 196; (1981) 206
Yardley, Bruce (1978) 126, 128; (1981) 197
Yashpal Sharma (1981/82) 197

Zaheer Abbas (1974) 44, 55; (1977/78) 111,
    131; (1978) 144